SELF-ENVY

Therapy and the
Divided Internal World

Rafael E. López Corvo

JASON ARONSON INC.
Northvale, New Jersey
London

This book was set in 10 point Bookman by TechType of Upper Saddle River, New Jersey, and printed and bound by Haddon Craftsmen of Scranton, Pennsylvania.

The author gratefully acknowledges permission to reprint the following:

A version of Chapter 3 was previously published in *Melanie Klein and Object Relations* 11: 1–94, 1993, and is reprinted by permission of the Ontario Institute for Studies in Education.

Sessions A and B in Chapter 7 were previously published in the *International Journal of Psycho-Analysis* 73: 719–728, 1993, and are reprinted by permission of the Institute of Psycho-Analysis.

Library of Congress Cataloging-in-Publication Data

López-Corvo, Rafael E.
    Self-envy / Rafael E. López-Corvo.
        p. cm.
    Includes bibliographical references and index.
    ISBN 1-56821-252-6
    1. Self-defeating behavior. 2. Borderline personality disorder—
Treatment. 3. Splitting (Psychology). 4. Envy. I. Title.
RC455.4.S43L67   1994
616.89—dc20   94-7733

Manufactured in the United States of America. Jason Aronson Inc. offers books and cassettes. For information and catalog write to Jason Aronson Inc., 230 Livingstone Street, Northvale, New Jersey 07647.

To
Alexander,
Vanessa,
and
Joanna

Contents

Preface   **ix**

Acknowledgments   **xiii**

1. Self-Envy   **1**

Creativity, Reparation and Self-Envy   10
Self-Reproach or Self-Envy?   22

**2. Splitting: The Psychology
   of Multiple Egos**   **27**

Splitting in Freud   29
Splitting versus Repression   35
Splitting after Freud: Object Relations Theory   43
Normal and Pathological Splitting   46
Splitting of Time   52
Splitting and Integration   53
Nothingness and Otherness   55

Contents

3. **Defensive Splitting
    and Schizoid Phenomena**   **61**

    The Schizoid Phenomena   63
    Quantitative (Depression) and Qualitative (Schizoid
        Phenomena) Aspects of Disturbed Mother–Child
        Natural Symbiosis   66
    Mother's Cultural Background and Schizoid
        Phenomena: Predominance of Obsessive Defenses
        in Anglo-Saxon Mothers and Phobic (Avoidance)
        Defenses in Latino Mothers   68

4. **Destructive Narcissism: Fusion
    versus Idealization**   **89**

    Destructive Narcissism   91
    Perverse and Destructive Narcissism   100

5. **Orestes versus Oedipus**   **111**

    Libido Contra Aggression   113
    Orestes versus Oedipus   122

6. **Revengeful versus Depressive Hope**   **125**

    Basic Delusion, Indispensability (Exception),
        and Revengeful Hope   127
    The Case of Hanna   131

7. **Borderline Structures and Mechanisms
    of Self-Envy**   **145**

    Case 1   151
    Case 2   157
    Case 3   166
    Case 4   174
    Self-Envy and Acting Out   176

Contents

8. **Self-Envy and Intrapsychic Interpretation**   **183**

    The Three Phases of Interpretation   185
    Clinical Material   192
    Summary   204

Epilogue   **207**

References   **213**

Index   **223**

Preface

"Why is it so difficult to talk about self-envy?" questioned Clifford Scott (1975, p. 336). The answer, as it turns out, is not straightforward, though it may be related to the difficulty of envisioning an internal world structured by infinite part object and part self-representations, interacting within the boundaries of the self. "Object relations theory," says Kernberg (1980) "examines metapsychology and clinical issues in terms of the vicissitudes of internalized object relations. Object relations theory considers the psychic apparatus as originating in the earliest stage of a sequence of internalization of object relations" (p. 17). Only when we conceive the internal world as the product of these long-introjected complex interactions of different and polyvalent self parts, can we understand that a despondent aspect of ourselves could envy another idealized or creative internal element.

We know since Freud that the characters populating dreams are no more than the invention of our inner unconscious fantasies. They may appear capable of independent action; but what they say and do, and what happens to them are absolutely our own invention. But if within the scenario of a dream, dream characters do appear to sustain a life of their own, why is it so difficult to imagine that different part self-objects could also behave in a similar fashion? A dream is, after all, only the visual and symbolic transcript of multiple unconscious condensations that push their way in as we sleep to convey a message to the awakened part of the self. Why are we so ready to declare ourselves absolute owners and possessors of our whole complicated and mysterious existence? I recall a young male obsessive patient with anal traits, who, at the beginning of his analysis, remained silent for the first ten minutes of every session. This was an obscure resistance that was understood one day when he mentioned that he was angry at himself because the night before, while talking to his girlfriend, he inadvertently called her "Mom." Rather upset, he speculated about how a part of himself could have done something like that if he was completely certain that he had resolved his "mother complex." In another words, he resented feeling betrayed by a slip of the tongue, because such a mistake made him feel that he didn't have complete control of himself, unlike the situation at the beginning of every session, when he examined all his words before he would even pronounce them, to make sure that there were no surprises, that he had a good "oral sphincter," and was in full command of his whole being.

It may be that we cannot quite fathom the depth and scope of the phenomenon of "splitting" or its importance in understanding unconscious phantasy, the complex interaction of projective and introjective identifications, the value of countertransference in making sense of latent content, or the way interpretations are fabricated.

So I will begin by introducing splitting immediately following the first chapter. Chapter 3 then deals with the notion of "schizoid phenomena," that is, how the personality organizes itself according to experiences in the individual's childhood that have induced splitting, touching on differences in social factors between Anglo-Saxon and Latin American cultures. Chapter 4 discusses the importance of narcissism, the multiple confusions that still exist in psychoanalytical metapsychology between the expansive quality resulting from identification with "object libido" or the "ideal object," as well as the phenomenon of "fusionability" in narcissistic relationships. Chapters 5 and 6 deal with the notion of death instinct, another significant concept that is still, like splitting, very controversial, although indispensable for understanding the dynamics of self-envy, further discussion of which follows in Chapter 7. The final chapter deals with the concept of "intrapsychic interpretation" as a different approach from the well-known spheres of extratransference and transference interpretation.

My hope is that this contribution may prove helpful to those dealing with relevant clinical problems that come up in daily therapeutic work with borderline patients, such as acting out, negative therapeutic reaction, addiction, perverse transference collusion, and so forth.

Acknowledgments

I am very grateful to my friend and teacher Dr. Clifford M. Scott, for his generous correspondence on the subject of self-envy, as well as his encouragement about investigating new ideas, and to my friend Dr. Jorge Ahumada, for his assistance and many suggestions in relation to the original publication of Chapter 7. I am also very much indebted to Dr. Guillermo Teruel, my training analyst, for introducing me to psychoanalysis, to my wife Anamilagros Pérez Morazzani for her infinite patience, and to my friends Lilian Reyna and Antonieta Isava for their unconditional assistance.

1

Self-Envy

As a dog was crossing a river with a piece of meat in his mouth, he saw, as he thought, another dog under the water with a bigger piece of meat upon the very same adventure. He never considered that one was only the image of the other; but, out of the desire to get the bigger piece, he jumped at the shadow and lost both, one because it did not exist, and the other because it was carried away by the current.

Aesop: "The Dog and His Shadow"

CREATIVITY AND SELF-ENVY

Born of humble origins in 1912 in the small Italian town of Forno di Canale, austere and extremely honest all of his life, Albino Luciani, entered the seminary at the age of 11, became a priest in 1935, a doctorate magna cum laude in theology when he was 34, the bishop of Vittorio Veneto in

1958, and finally pope on August 26, 1978, with the name of John Paul I. His death on September 28, exactly thirty-two days later, was so appalling and unbelievable that some began to suspect foul play. Following this line of thinking, David Yallop wrote a very popular account, *In God's Name,* speculating about a complicated plot conceived by other cardinals at the Vatican, who for one reason or another might have been unhappy with Luciani's nomination. Such speculations do not merit any serious consideration; Luciani most likely died of natural causes.[1] But if this is in fact the case, how are we to understand that after achieving such a high position in his profession, someone like Luciani could just suddenly die?

If Luciani's history seems sad, consider that of Tancredo de Almeida Neves, a Brazilian lawyer graduated in 1932, who had a brilliant and fast-moving career as a politician: deputy to the Parliament since 1950, appointed minister of justice in 1953, then elected senator in 1978, governor for the state of Minas Gerais in 1982, and finally president of Brazil on January 15, 1985. "Kind, elegant, capable of finding those points of agreement when disagreement was imminent, always present in difficult hours, he became a specialist in the therapy of political crisis."[2] He worked so hard all his life as a politician to become president of Brazil that it is paradoxical, and devoid of any simple logic, that on March 14, exactly on the eve of his inauguration, Tancredo Neves was hospitalized

---

[1] A similar history was that of Alessandro de' Medici, who became Pope Leo XI, after Clement VII's death, on April 1, 1605, and died twenty-six days later, on the 27th of the same month.

[2] *Veja, Suplemento historico* no. 869, Brazil, p. 3.

with septicemia, that is, a generalized infection, and that a week later he was dead. How do we explain such an incongruity?

Similar incongruities abound in the lives of other notables. An ancient stone found in Greece carries the following message: "Homer equals blind," meaning perhaps that either the word *Homer* signified *blind*, or that Homer, the great epic writer, was sightless. Most investigators have inclined toward the latter, believing that the paradox of the blind writer was already known in those early times. The Irish novelist James Joyce not only identified himself with Homer by writing his best seller *Ulysses* as a new version of the *Odyssey*, but once said that his eye troubles were produced by a glaucoma *foudroyant*, the same disease that blinded Homer, according to Joyce (Ellmann 1982). "Ce qu'apportent les yeux n'est rien. J'ai cent mondes a créer, je n'en perds qu'un,"[3] remarked Joyce once to a friend, spontaneously linking his malaise with his creativity (Ellmann 1982, p. 664). A similar fate befell Argentinean author Jorge Luis Borges, who died not long ago after many years of complete blindness, as did his fellow countryman Ernesto Sabato. Sabato not only became blind very recently but also uncannily wrote, long before the disease caught up with him, his well-known story "Informe sobre los Ciegos,"[4] a detailed account of the subculture and everyday life of blind people.

Another paradigm is that of a paradoxical combination of great ingenuity, on the one hand, and a complete

---

[3]"What the eyes bring is nothing. I have a hundred worlds to create, I am losing only one of them."
[4]"Information about the Blind."

loss of the specific and requisite sense needed to produce and sustain creativity, on the other. I think of Ludwig van Beethoven, one of the greatest composers of the last century, who also became completely deaf. What could be more ironic than a blind writer or a deaf composer? From the histories presented here, one might think that all these persons shared a tragic fate in common, that they were doomed by pure bad luck or condemned by random forces of destiny. However, I want to introduce a different hypothesis: that possibly a part of them played a bad trick in their own minds, an unconscious machination against success, guided by feelings of destructive envy or self-envy in an inner struggle within the self. Let us examine the case of Beatriz in an attempt to clarify these concepts.

Beatriz is a 25-year-old single architect who consulted because of low self-esteem and great difficulty establishing lasting relationships with males. She was the youngest of four sisters, all married and living on their own, while Beatriz was still living with her mother. Her parents were divorced when she was around 10 years of age, and she grew up feeling that she was treated by her older sisters as if she was a source of continuous irritation, a real "pest," as she herself expressed it. The belief that she was not physically attractive and that she could not make anybody happy surfaced in the transference as a tendency to apologize for whatever she had to say, or to find it very difficult to express her thoughts. Her main concern was her difficulties with men. She followed the pattern of rejecting those who were interested in her and desiring those she felt rejected her. She remembered how her sisters, her girlfriends, even her divorced mother, had no trouble at all in finding boyfriends. Although she is an attractive girl, she considered herself very plain in comparison with her sisters, a belief that generated important feelings of envy toward them, which she displaced to many of her girlfriends. Very often there was an unconscious need to create a triangular relationship, and she became interested in men who were usually involved with other women. At a given moment we were able to find a symbolic association with Snow White's stepmother, who continuously questioned her mirror to find out who was most beautiful. It was as if Beatriz needed men to assure her that her suspicions that no one wanted her were not true. Early work in her analysis about her oedipal rivalry with her mother and sisters over her father's love and attention managed to help her to establish, for the first time, a worthwhile relationship with Felipe, a former friend: "someone I knew for many years, just as a friend," although now she has discovered that they have many things in common and that she is capable of experiencing "a lot of chemistry towards him." During the last two weeks the material of her sessions had been exclusively about Felipe: about how envious her girlfriends might be, fear that he could reject her or think that she is not attractive enough, how much she loves him, how grateful she feels about the analysis because she feels different, and so on. She continually remarked on this difference in her feelings, how new it all was for her, how much she cared for Felipe, and how she thought of him every minute.

Following a terrorist attempt on a Saturday morning in which an employee in a parking lot was killed, Beatriz had the following dream that same night: *She was at her house and a common friend of both of them called saying that something terrible had happened to Felipe, that he was trapped during a bomb explosion. Beatriz kept desperately asking what exactly had happened to him, but her friend kept talking, implying that something had happened to Felipe, but never saying exactly what.* Beatriz woke up in a state of great anxiety.

There were in the "sleeping part of Beatriz" an infinite number of possibilities for concocting a happy and pleasant dream—that she and Felipe got married, for instance, or that her sisters were dying with envy, that she won first prize, or whatever. However, she chose the most frightening situation she could: that her sweetheart, the first man she had ever loved, was in terrible danger, perhaps even dead. Why? Just like Tancredo Neves, Albino Luciani, Beethoven, Borges, or Joyce, Beatriz has chosen the path of tragedy instead of happiness and complete success. It seemed to me that there were at least two Beatrizes, or two part self-objects: on the one hand, there was the "youngest-envious-sister part" who felt, or was convinced, that the capacity to develop a loving relationship with men was something completely foreign to her and only belonged to others—to her sisters or her mother; on the other hand, there was another Beatriz, a new one, who, like her mother and sisters, had now managed for the first time to initiate the same kind of relationship that only they were capable of or had the prerogative to initiate. The envy that Beatriz had felt toward her mother and sisters before was now introjected and exercised against another part of herself, who, like her sisters, was capable of developing the same kind or loving relationship with men. In other words, there was a "pest part" of Beatriz who envied the part of Beatriz "in love with Felipe," just as she felt her sisters and mother used to do.

Finally, in this short list of outstanding masters, exceptional virtuosos, and everyday people, Stephen Hawking comes to mind, that contemporary clear-minded physicist who has made an exceptional effort to introduce us neophytes into the complicated field of infinitude, endless time, light-year velocity, and the like, and who has at the same time, curiously, become paralyzed. How can we understand such a disparity, such a puzzling combination in the same person of a particular and intense dedication to study the unimaginable and complete corporal immobility?

Amyotrophic lateral sclerosis (ALS)—Stephen Hawking's illness—and rheumatoid arthritis (RA) are two degenerative diseases of unknown etiology with differing prognoses. ALS is deadly; RA is not. They have in common only a progressive limitation of movement. I have never treated a person with ALS, but I have seen patients with arthritis. I particularly remember a middle-aged woman I saw for about six months for a crisis intervention. She had developed an acute and severe case of arthritis following her husband's sudden death about a month previously. The most important aspect of her anxiety, which ameliorated after she developed the arthritis, was her extreme guilt about being alive, her secret and manic triumph over the dead object. Once she understood this mechanism, her limitation improved. The arthritis represented an envious part self-object in her that identified with the dead object and furiously attacked her capacity to move as an expression of being alive.

CREATIVITY, REPARATION AND SELF-ENVY

Up to this point I have referred only to creative individuals who suffered some kind of physical ailment, or unwillingly lost their lives. I have also introduced the hypothesis that the nature of their affliction leads to the suspicion that there may exist an unconscious and direct relationship between such disorders and these people's creative capacities. The unconscious linkage between the symptom and the particular act of creation is produced by a mechanism of self-envy—the envy produced between an excluded part and a creative part of the self.

Now I wish to introduce another side of the same subject, something already referred to by Aristotle, who once declared that there was a clear relation between poetry and melancholy, or, expressed in more general terms, that creative people very often suffer from significant mental derangement. I can think of Van Gogh, Baudelaire, Coleridge, Poe, Lord Byron, Robert Louis Stevenson, Conan Doyle, Schumann, Virginia Woolf, Aldous Huxley, and Hemingway, just to mention a few of those individuals who have made themselves a significant place in history but who were also host to serious mental conflicts, alcohol or drug addiction, suicide, or other forms of violent death. How could one person shelter at the same time such a high level of sensitivity and creativity together with so much suffering and madness? How could such creative individuals at the same time be so destructive?

A psychoanalytical interest in creativity has existed since Freud, who wrote several essays on the subject, such

10

as "Creative Writers and Day-Dreaming" (1908), "Leonardo da Vinci and a Memory of His Childhood" (1910), "The Theme of the Three Caskets" (1913). "We laymen have always wondered greatly—like the cardinal who put the question to Ariosto—how that strange being, the poet, comes by his material," wrote Freud in 1908 (p. 141), associating creativity with unconscious fantasies and daydreaming activity, a position also sustained by Winnicott (1951) who emphasized the relationship between creativity and children's play. Kohut (1971), on the other hand, points out the importance of narcissistic exhibitionism present in any work of art, and its relation to sublimation or neutralization of "formerly frozen narcissistic cathexes in the area of both grandiose self and the idealized parent imago" (p. 308). Kleinians prefer to use reparation instead of sublimation as employed in the classical approach for the same reason that the former also favored splitting over repression, as I will discuss in the next chapter. The differences between sublimation and repression on one side, and splitting and reparation on the other, hinge on how the unconscious was conceived by different schools of psychoanalysis, mainly ego psychology and object relations theories: drive, instincts, or impulses for the former and object representations for the latter. In this sense it would be easier to speak in terms of repression or sublimation of a drive as well as splitting and reparation of the object.

Hanna Segal (1981) believes that creativity is a re-creation of a once loved and total object that had been lost and ruined along with the internal world that is then brought back to life by the existence of depressive phantasies that induce the act of creativity, consisting of infusing "life into dead fragments," or re-creating life. In summary, the artistic work could be considered as "a way of working through the depressive position." She said:

> The memory of the good situation, where the infant's ego contained the whole loved object and the realization that it has been lost through his own attacks, give rise to an intense feeling of loss and guilt, and to the wish to restore and re-create the lost loved object outside and within the ego. This wish to restore and re-create is the basis of later sublimation and creativity. . . . The task of the artist lies in the creation of a world of his own. . . . [pp. 187–188]

Where there is a significant amount of psychopathology present, there is the successive alternation of suffering and creative production, where the continuous creation represents a failing attempt to repair the internal representation of a damaged object. In this attempt there is a successive chain of events that begins with the need to establish a narcissistic fusion with the ideal object, as well as the expansive exhibitionism that goes with it. In the second place, there is also a necessity to repair this object, believed to damaged during the previous act of narcissistic fusion. The main difficulty, however, is the failure of this undertaking and the need to repeat again and again the same attempts and failures: narcissistic fusion, reparation, failure, loss of the object, anxiety, and need to search again for fusion with the lost idealized object. During the period of narcissistic fusion there is a manic symptomatology: exhibitionism, omnipotence, triumph, elation, and great creative production. This burst of energy is the antithesis of the periods of failure and loss of the idealized object, where depressive features such as hopelessness and total inhibition of creativity prevail.

What exactly is this failure at repairing the ideal object? What does it mean? How can we understand it? The main conflict is that once the ego experiences the elation induced by the narcissistic fusion with the longed-for ideal object within the self, powerful feelings of envy, or rather self-envy, from the representation of an excluded child–self object are then automatically triggered, and are experienced now in the same manner as they were perceived in childhood. This narcissistic combination of self and ideal object, experienced as a feeling of oneness within the self, induces a great amount of envy, similar to that experienced during childhood by the excluded child toward the harmonious parental couple. It seems as if those aspects that are envied and consequently attacked (failure of the process of reparation), remain inside the self as narcissistic identifications that are never recognized by the self as its own, but are experienced instead as foreign bodies, similar to the mechanism observed in diseases of the immune system, such as lupus erythematosus or diabetes, where certain cells of the body are treated as enemies and attacked by antibodies and immune complexes of the same organism. In the case of creativity, I believe that the failure of the process of reparation in these artists, where creativity alternates with a significant level of psychic pain, is a mechanism of *self-envy* experienced by an excluded part of the self against the act of reparation of the ideal object (fusion of self and ideal object representations), perceived as a foreign body because of a narcissistic identification. Creativity in these individuals is the consequence of a continuous failure of the act of sublimation, neutralization, or reparation, or the achievement of a depressive position due to a mechanism of self-envy.

The following case illustrates the importance of mother–child eye contact during breast feeding as an expression of narcissistic fusion with the ideal object. Nancy, a patient in analysis for the last three years, diagnosed as a narcissistic personality, presented a history of severe early deprivation related in great part to her position as an older sibling followed at nine month intervals by eight more children. There was a history of child molestation by her maternal grandfather consisting of caressing, fondling, and masturbation, and later also when she was 6 years old, by a gambler who often visited her house. For many years the transference was centered mainly around her need to re-create the envious and destructive masturbatory couple as a tight narcissistic interaction, perverse in nature, that gave no alternative but to be repeated again and again in the transference in order to achieve satisfaction, or to experience with destructive anger the abstinence of the analytical situation. A manic defense served the purpose of concealing the pain experienced as a child when the mother slowly slipped away after each birth of the other siblings.

She attended analysis four times weekly, at the same late-afternoon hour, except for Wednesdays, when she was the first morning patient. This was a Wednesday session. Nancy started complaining about the analysis—as she had done several times during the previous three months— how she was fed up talking about the same things; that the analyst was too distant; that she knew all the whys and all the answers, but none of this helped her. Since she was tired of talking to herself, she felt compelled to stop coming altogether. After a short pause she said that it had been so different the day before, when she went to visit some people because of an investigation she was conducting on the subject of several houses built by an architect now deceased. She went to visit these houses and the occupants were extremely pleasant and warm. In one of the houses, the first one she visited, the gentleman who opened the door spent the whole morning showing the house to her, and she noted how strange the windows were—"like eyes looking outside. I think that those windows shaped like eyes were constructed just to look outside." From there she went to another house, occupied this time by the architect's widow, who was also very nice and didn't want Nancy to leave.

Countertransferentially I also felt "fed up," and rather angry that she was again complaining about the same things, instead of working in alliance with me. Since my office is in my house, I felt that perhaps she was referring to her wish to see my house. However, at this particular moment, using my countertransference feelings, I decided to show her the contrast between her attitude and those of the people she had visited. I said to her that perhaps she was now expressing her great difficulty in showing me her inner house because of her anger, different from the attitude the people she had visited the day before had shown toward her. "The other days," she answered after a short pause, "are very different from today, Wednesday; on Wednesday you seem more fresh, more sharp. Perhaps the other sessions, which are during the afternoon, you are tired; but Wednesday is a different day, and also because the hour remains permanent, always the same time since I started the analysis, different from the other hours, which have changed. Perhaps, like you said, it is difficult for me to show you my house, different from what the people I visited did with me. In the widow's house, which is a very old one, there were several boxes filled with documents and old pictures. It was like a treasure—paintings from the sixteenth century, even a picture painted by Raphael; and this architect I am researching, I think that he was a genius. He was very sure of himself and he did whatever he wanted, without ever minding about other people's opinions, and that is why the house is so strange. His wife told me that for a while she put it on sale, and the people who came to see it left in terror . . . what I think happens to me here is that I feel like a beggar, begging for love, that you would listen to me, and would talk to me like those people from the houses just did, and that at the end of the hour, you wouldn't dismiss me.''

Then I said: ''Perhaps your concern about sharing your inner self with me results from the fear that if we were to open those old boxes inside of you, many old and sad memories would appear, and we would be so sad that I might leave in terror; but also it seems that next to this sad beggar that frightens you so much, there is also a great treasure and a great creativity. That there are things that will never change and will always keep their value, like Wednesdays or Raphael's paintings. Perhaps this is related to the fact that you feel you are the first patient today, so you will be able to get fresh and sharp interpretations, like fresh milk from a fresh mother who has not yet conceived other babies, different from the other days, when you feel my breast is withered after so many patient-brothers and sisters, just as might have happened in your real life when you were born.''

As I spoke she started to cry; then she said that her mother was in town from the interior, where she lives, and that she feels very angry at her. Nancy had asked her to come to her house, but her mother said that she will only go where she is invited. The other day she was with her mother and two of her sisters, and one of them said to her, "Well, Nancy, you are the oldest one, and that is something that is never lost. You will always be the oldest." "The first child," Nancy continued, "is an experience that is never forgotten; it is something unique; only someone who has been a mother knows the experience of having a baby inside." Then after a long pause she made a remark about something she had described previously. She said that while she was talking her lips protruded as if she were sucking, so much so that she had trouble articulating, and that this happens sometimes when she feels upset. (From my seat I could see what she meant; her lips were protruding continuously as if she were really sucking.) After another pause she said that suddenly, she didn't know why, the memory of a song she knew when she was around 5 years old came to her mind. She remembered the age because she didn't yet know how to write, and it was so important for her, this song, that she asked a cousin to write the words down. It went: "Your green eyes, green, green, like the green sea." She didn't know why the song was so important to her. Her husband has green eyes, as well as her oldest daughter, who is very special to her because of the color of her eyes, and her mother also has green eyes. Perhaps the color of her mother's eyes has been very important for her without her realizing it. "And my eyes are black, but I must carry the gene inside because I had a green-eyed daughter." As she was

17

speaking I thought of the relationship to "green sea" as a symbol of the mother, and asked her if she knew what the baby sees when it is breast feeding, and she answered, "Yes, the mother's eyes."

Nancy was a successful professional: a university professor, author of several books, a sculptor recognized internationally, and was married with three children, with no other apparent difficulties. The contrast between the level and nature of her chronic anxiety and her capacity to perform academically in spite of all her suffering has always been a source of amazement to her. Her ambivalence about her need for affection and recognition, together with intense feelings of anger and revenge, colored the transference from the very beginning of her analysis. I thought that this last session revealed an important aspect in the reconstruction of her past, namely, the existence of an internal object or a particular condition responsible for her creativity. I thought that the symbolism present in this session was like a window to her past: the windows resembling eyes "looking outside," her admiration for the deceased architect, the consistency of Wednesdays as well as the value of Raphael's pictures (Rafael is also my name), and in spite of the sad memories, the sudden association with the song about the green eyes and their importance in relation to her mother, husband, and oldest daughter; and most of all, the protruding, sucking-like movement of her lips. All of this made me think of the placidity and undisturbed condition of a baby sucking the mother's breast while directly looking at her green eyes, and suddenly one day (just nine months later), the disruption of the relationship with the advent of a new child. A condition that was present also in the transference as well as in the countertransference was seen at the beginning of this session when she complained about the frustration she experienced due to the analytical abstinence.

Was this the exact sequence of all of these events? Did they really happen in the way I have just described? We will never really know, because we only have theoretical conjecture that can never be proved. The process will be compulsively repeated, its meaning deeply repressed. Perhaps some day, it will even be properly named and become conscious, but that is all. It will never portray the exact physiognomy of the original fact. In the session described, there is a somatic language: the protruding lips, which offer more credibility than the manifest discourse, because symptoms of this category, closely linked and supported by a biological substratum are a better representation of truth, like the transference that always represents a faithful translator of the real fact. The discourse is also very important because how the chain of associations and automatic flow of symbolic representations were articulated during the session repeats the spontaneous order of cathexis. This is why I considered the association of the song about the green eyes and the windows resembling eyes as a possible expression of the scoptophilic interest of a baby in the mother's eyes at the moment of breast feeding. This last hypothesis is introduced from my own spontaneous countertransference phantasy.

During another session, a few days later, she spoke again about how important it was for her to look at and to be looked at by other men "like a form of comunication." "A complicity?" I asked. "No," she denied, and insisted that it was instead, a form of exchange or comunication. "To look around," she continued, "is a very important form of comunication, mostly with men. The other day I was driving and I saw a man with green eyes walking by, and the immediate feeling was to follow him. It's like something mysterious and very powerful. In the kind of work that I do looking is essential. When I travel I take many pictures of buildings. I look for how the artist's presence is manifested in his creation, even more, to try to find out about others who have influenced the artist, how well executed the work is and how it relates to the background."

Like her investigation into the houses of the deceased architect, she searched for the presence of an absence, for her mother, whose presence diminished after each pregnancy, with the green eyes the only invariable factor indicating her presence, or through the transference on Wednesdays. It was the mother's identity that she had searched continuously for in the profiles of those foreign buldings captured by her camera.

A few days later, she said that her printer had gone absolutely crazy, that it did not respond to the conformation provided by her computer and "is printing backwards and does not follow the instructions." She remembered a dream: *She was wearing working clothes and was with a girl friend at her art gallery's office. Then she was in a bus with several male managers from a fishery who were driving down to the beach to fish. When they arrived, she explained to them that she had a new method for fishing and asked to be tied and lowered into the water. Underneath the water it was fantastic. All kinds of fish flew to the net and stuck to it by the thousands until she gave indication to be raised. After the fishing was concluded, she demanded that 70 percent of the profits be given to her. A great argument with the owners ensued until finally they decided not to use her, and she woke up.*

She remembered the argument from last week's session, when she felt fine in the morning before coming, but felt bad after she had left. She thought that the bus with the managers represented the analysis, and submerging under the water to fish might have something to do with the work we were doing. I felt that the first part of the dream represented the good disposition she had before coming for her session: to be in her "working clothes" at her creative office, in a creative frame of mind. Then she wanted to help, to get involved in the process of discovery, of fishing for and revealing the unconscious, but at a given moment something happened and the initial cooperation was changed into an envious competition: she wanted 70 percent and this became unworkable, as if an envious part of herself could not abide the possibility that another aspect of herself could have been so cooperative in the analytical process. After all, why would she demand such a high amount? Why not a more workable percentage that could have allowed her to continue sleeping, fabricating dreams, fishing, and preserving the partnership? This dream seems to summarize the main conflict present in the transference: a desire to establish a profitable and creative working alliance (wearing working clothes, fishing), that immediately triggers envious feelings from an excluded child part (unworkable partnership of 70 percent), that has lost its mother because of seven more siblings, and then, the appearance of the masturbatory, symbiotic, and destructive part, which, by means of self-envy mechanisms (doing all the fishing alone) attacks her creative attempt, and a profitable communication is lost

21

because the alienated-self-printer, out of envy, goes "absolutely crazy" and does not respond to its alliance with the analyst-computer.

Although I am only presenting one case, in order to psychoanalytically evaluate the relation between psychopathology and creativity, I think that this mechanism could be easily observed during the analysis of creative persons who, at the same time, experience an important amount of psychopathology such as bipolar symptomatology.

SELF-REPROACH OR SELF-ENVY?

In 1916 Freud referred in his paper "Those Wrecked by Success" to certain patients who

> occasionally fall ill precisely when a deeply-rooted and long cherished wish has come to fulfillment. It seems as though they were not able to tolerate their happiness; for there can be no question that there is a causal connection between their success and their falling ill. . . . Psychoanalytic work teaches that the forces of conscience which induce illness in consequence of success, instead of, as normally, in consequence of frustration, are closely connected with the Oedipus Complex. [p. 331]

While Klein (1963) goes a bit further than Freud and seems to reach very close to the concept of self-envy, she does not elaborate and the notion remains implicit: for instance, she makes reference to "the envious and destructive attack against the mother's fertility" but does not specify the envious attack on this object once it has been introjected. She states:

> The infantile anxiety lest triumph over others and destruction of their capacities make them envious and dangerous has important consequences in later life. Some people deal with this anxiety by inhibiting their own gifts. Freud (1916) has described a type of individual who cannot bear success because it arouses guilt, and he connected this guilt in particular with the Oedipus complex. In my view, such people originally meant to outshine and destroy the mother's fertility. Some of these feelings are transferred to the father and to siblings, and later on to other people whose envy and hate are then feared; guilt in this connection may lead to strong inhibitions of talent and potentialities. [p. 281]

According to this account, all of the cases I have just described have developed an important ego incongruity as a consequence of guilt produced by the realization of unconscious oedipal desires. I do believe that perhaps this might well be the mechanism in those cases where creativity appears inhibited; that is, a strong superego threat will not allow the ego to develop constructive tendencies because they might hide unconscious incestuous as well as parricidal or matricidal dispositions. I am now introducing another possibility, that a "child part self-object" that remains separated (split off) will exercise destructive and envious feelings against the "creative aspects of the self," which already exist and have been used industriously, but are now attacked out of envious feelings when identified as another separated self-object.

In 1975, in discussing dreams, Scott introduced the

concept of the *self-envy* mechanism in a short account that unfortunately he failed to elaborate further. Self-envy is present, he said, "whenever a conflict exists between a depreciated aspect and an idealizing aspect of what becomes a whole continuing ego" (p. 336).

Recently (1992) I also described self-envy as

> the envious attack by a part of the self, usually related to childhood self-objects, against another part of the self identified as a creative and harmonious mother–father or parent–sibling relationship, also within the self, which is now transferentially projected as a means of avoiding superego accusations. [p. 720]

Feelings of self-reproach—that is, guilt induced by superego attack—and self-envy may at times be difficult to discriminate, although from a theoretical point of view they are forces or energies coming from opposite directions. Self-reproach is the consequence of superego attack against the ego, experienced as feelings of guilt because of destructive oedipal fantasies; self-envy results from direct attack of aggressive drives emanating from a now introjected part object, originally experienced outside, against another part object.

Diana, a 45-year-old female professional, to whom I will be referring in detail at the end of this book, had managed after four years of analysis to achieve some success as a researcher at the university where she teaches, as well as publish several papers. It was clear that her inhibition was due to feelings of guilt and fear of retaliation; lately, however, a self-envy mechanism had became more obvious, and we had been working in this direction. At her first session on returning from a one-week holiday, she started by describing certain difficulties she had when dealing with a government office in order to obtain funds to continue her research. She accused herself of not doing enough, of leaving things for the last minute, of not keeping records of what she had done. She said that she was lucky that she ended up getting more money from the government than she expected; she said also that though she did not prepare herself well for the congress, at the end she was congratulated by her colleagues for the paper she had presented. Then she referred to a "long and complicated" dream she had the night before in which she did more or less the same things she had just told me about but in a different manner, because she was facing endless complications and inconveniences that kept her from being able to achieve what she wanted. At a given moment she could not find the government office, and the person she had to talk to wasn't there; afterward she could not deliver her paper, as she had spent all her time looking for the location of the congress but could not find it. Then she said that before, things were the opposite—she couldn't do anything in her real life, but she dreamed about doing it. However, now that she is able to achieve and enjoys it, she dreams about failure.

I thought that before she used to envy what others created outside and wanted to destroy it. She had managed in her analysis to deal with this conflict and had identified herself with the creative part that she had previously projected onto others. Now the envy continues inside of her and is manifested in the attack that a part of her makes in her dreams against her creative realization, spoiling her achievements and inducing anxiety. At the beginning of the session a demanding superego aspect, never satisfied with whatever she accomplishes, accused her of not doing things right, of not doing enough. This, I think, represents feelings of self-reproach, while the inversion of reality in the dream, where a difficulty is powerfully established in order to sabotage her achievements, is self-envy.

2

Splitting: The Psychology of Multiple Egos

SPLITTING IN FREUD

It is impossible to grasp the notion of self-envy without considering the existence of a divided self, of multiple interacting egos—the product of the mind's tendency to split as an important form of defense or a biological need to excrete unpleasant feelings that threaten to overwhelm the baby's frail and primitive ego. But this primitive self is by nature inchoately divided, as if we were born in pieces and will progressively, as we grow, change into a universal world, into a more integrated self. Perhaps cognitive experimentation, as carried out by Piaget and his collaborators, is generally more explicit about this early and standard splitting of the self than investigations effected on the emotional side have disclosed. We will return later to this subject of "cognitive splitting."

If it is difficult to confess to envy, it is even more difficult to apprehend the existence of envy against other feelings harbored within the same person, regardless of the fact that envy, like beauty, is also in the eye of the beholder. Envy is to projection what self-envy is to introjection, where the field of action has changed from the range of the outside objects to the inner limits of the internal world. Thus self-envy usually refers to outside objects or situations envied during childhood, later introjected, and now interacting still as foreign objects but inside the self, as an "orbital identification," to use Wisdom's (1961) expression. Emotions that were ours once, spurred from the core of our innermost self, that were then split off and later projected, become foreign, completely estranged, unrecognizable—after all, what we envy is exactly what we lack. Yet these same alienated experiences, if reintrojected or recognized as ours, will always elicit reactions ranging from fright to depression to a complete psychotic break depending, of course, on the individual ego's resources.

The different forms of splitting, as well as the changes resulting from the whole phenomenology of splitting, will determine the diagnosis of mental states, changing from slow and large split portions of the self, as seen in neurotic patients, to fast and minute split parts, observed in psychotics. This former mechanism of splitting, some authors such as Bion (1967) and Grotstein (1986) have referred to as dissociation, leaving the concept of splitting proper to the later psychotic mechanisms.

Splitting, then, is an important defense that we will investigate further in order to clarify the description of the self-envy mechanism. However, since this concept evolved late in psychoanalysis, we can evaluate its dynamics from two different perspectives, either as a historical evolution or by considering the specific mechanism responsible for the process of splitting. Since I have chosen the first approach, we will begin with Freud and leave the other aspect for the next chapter.

Although Freud conceived of splitting early on, it did not evolve until late in his life, due perhaps to the influence the mechanism of the "steam-engine model," based on accumulation and release of pressure, had during these early stages of psychoanalytical discoveries; it was also easier at the time, following that same influence, to talk about "repression of the instinct" than "splitting of self and object."

The continuous progress of psychoanalytical theory and practice, on the other hand, from Freud to Klein and further on to Bion, could be compared to the change in magnification of the microscope's objective lenses, changing from "dissociation" in Freud, to "splitting of the parts" in Klein and finally to Bion's "splitting of particles."

Splitting, in German, *Spaltung*, was not a concept originally restricted to the field of psychoanalysis. It was widely used in psychiatry by Janet and Bleuler, among others, as "splitting of consciousness" *(Bewusstseinsspaltung)*, synonymous with "double consciousness," "dissociation," or "split personality." The meaning I will use here, however, was introduced for the first time by Freud rather late, in dealing with the concept of disavowal and fetishism.[1]

---

[1]Although Strachey warns us about Freud's statement being fanciful, I do not agree with his account in relation to Freud's paper on fetishism (see footnote in Freud [1921], p. 151), that the notion of "splitting of the ego" elaborated by Freud in this paper

In 1894, in his article "Neuro-Psychoses of Defense," Freud stated:

> Since the fine work done by Pierre Janet, Josef Breuer and others, it may be taken as generally recognized that the syndrome of hysteria, so far as it is as yet intelligible, justifies the assumption of there being a splitting of consciousness accompanied by the formation of separate psychical groups. Opinions are less settled, however, about the origin of this splitting of consciousness and about the part played by this characteristic in the structure of the hysterical neurosis. [pp. 45–46]

It is obvious that at this early stage in the history of psychoanalysis, Freud was dealing with psychic structures more from a clinical and phenomenological point of view than from a metapsychological one, metapsychology being still too far ahead in the line of his future discoveries. Splitting was at this time strictly connected with dissociated states of consciousness, similar to the notion put forth by Janet, with the difference that for him splitting was primary and inherited, whereas for Freud it was the opposite: a condition acquired and secondary to a "dreamlike state of consciousness" that interfered with thought association and was a common symptom among hysterical patients. It is interesting that Freud laid aside the notion of splitting for the next thirty years. When he came back to it in 1924, he saw it as an intrasystemic mechanism rather than as a state of consciousness. Perhaps the need to build

---

was already in his mind back in 1896 at the time of the "Project"; otherwise, why would he insist in 1938 that the notion of splitting he was then introducing was a completely new concept?

the scaffolding for psychoanalytical theory and practice was behind his conceiving a different kind of splitting, such as that between agencies—ego and id or ego and superego—or between unconscious, preconscious, and consciousness. In any event, a year after the conceptualization of the id, ego, and superego had been fully established, Freud (1924a) reintroduced the notion of splitting:

> One would like to know in what circumstances and by what means the ego can succeed in emerging from such conflicts, which are certainly always present, without falling ill. This is a new field of research, in which no doubt the most varied factors will come up for examination. Two of them, however, can be stressed at once. In the first place, the outcome of all such situations will undoubtedly depend on economic considerations—on the relative magnitudes of the trends which are struggling with one another. In the second place, it will be possible for the ego to avoid a rupture in any direction by deforming itself, by submitting to encroachments on its own unity and even perhaps be effecting cleavage or division of itself. In this way the inconsistencies, eccentricities and follies of men would appear in a similar light to their sexual perversions, through the acceptance of which they spare themselves repressions. [pp. 152–153]

With this new position Freud was placing himself quite a distance from "the facile formula that neuroses were the negative of perversions," according to Meltzer (1973).

But Freud hit on the true concept of splitting while investigating fetishism and psychosis in 1927, when he elaborated the similitude between the Rat Man's scotomization of his father's death and the disavowal *(Verleugnung)* fetishists develop because of their castration fears about women's absence of a penis. "It was only one current in their mental life that had not recognized their father's death; there was another current which took full account of that fact. The attitude which fitted in with the wish and the attitude which fitted in with reality existed side by side" (p. 156). In *An Outline of Psycho-Analysis* Freud (1940a) established that splitting was a more common defense than he had previously thought:

> The view which postulates that in all psychoses there is a *splitting of the ego* could not call for so much notice if it did not turn out to apply to other states more like the neuroses and finally, to the neuroses themselves. I first became convinced of this in cases of *fetishism* . . . The facts of this splitting of the ego, which we have just described, are neither so new nor so strange as they may at first appear. It is indeed a universal characteristic of neuroses that there are present in the subject's mental life, as regards some particular behavior, two different attitudes, contrary to each other and independent of each other. [pp. 202, 204]

Finally, in 1938, in a posthumously published paper (1940b) specifically devoted to subject of splitting, he wrote: "I find myself for a moment in the interesting position of not knowing whether what I have to say should be regarded as something long familiar and obvious or as something entirely new and puzzling. But I am inclined to think the latter" (pp. 275–278).

Writing near the end of his life, Freud did not extend himself further on this subject, finishing it inconclusively and leaving out, among other things, the interaction between splitting and other defense mechanisms such as repression. For Freud then, the expression *"splitting of the ego"* meant the existence of two opposite attitudes that exist side by side without ever influencing each other, as if one aspect did not wish to know about the other.

In summary, we can distinguish perhaps three different stages in the historical development of the concept of splitting in Freud: In the first stage splitting is not a metapsychological notion but related to clinical psychiatry and synonymous with "dissociation of consciousness," discussed mostly in his 1894 paper "Neuro-Psychosis of Defense," and perhaps also two years earlier, in Draft K of Freud's (1950) letters to Fliess in which Freud refers to a "malformation" or "alteration" of the ego. Publication of *Neurosis and Psychosis* in 1924, as well as *Fetishism* in 1927, initiates a second stage, in which "splitting of the ego" is associated with disavowal and perversion, on the one hand, and psychosis on the other. Finally in *Splitting of the Ego in the Process of Defense*, as well as in Chapter 8 of *An Outline of Psycho-Analysis*, both written in 1938, splitting is considered a universal form of ego defense, not just specific to psychosis and perversion but seen in neurosis as well, and this, I think, was what Freud had in mind when he alluded to splitting as a "new and puzzling" discovery.

SPLITTING VERSUS REPRESSION

In the preliminary communication of his 1893 *Studies in Hysteria*, Freud referred to repression as the unconscious motivation of hysterical patients to forget; in other words, the understanding of the mechanism during these early years was obviously analogous to hysterical amnesia, a concept reaffirmed again in 1926 in Chapter 11 of *Inhibition Symptoms and Anxiety*. In his 1915 article on repression, the essence of the concept was defined differently from that expressed in 1893, and was now described as the ego capacity to turn an instinctive wish away and to keep it "at a distance, from the conscious" (Freud 1915, pp. 141–158). In 1926 Freud also considered the relationship between repression and defense, two concepts he used synonymously for a long time, until the profusion of mechanisms—hysterical amnesia, of course, but also conversion, displacement in obsessive neurosis, and psychotic projection—persuaded him that defense was a more generalized concept than repression:

> It will be an undoubted advantage, I think, to revert to the old concept of "defence," provided we employ it explicitly as a general designation for all the techniques which the ego makes use of in conflicts which may lead to a neurosis, while we retain the word "repression" for the special method of defence which the line of approach taken by our investigations made us better acquainted with in the first instance. [p. 163]

In in his 1927 article on fetishism, Freud attempts to establish a difference between "repression" (*Verdrängung*) and disavowal (*Verleugnung*):

> If we wanted to differentiate more sharply between the vicissitude of the *idea* as distinct from that of the *affect*, and reserve the word "*Verdrängung*" "repres-

sion" for the affect, then the correct German word for the vicissitude of the idea would be "*Verleugnung*" "disavowal." "Scotomization" seems to me particularly unsuitable, for it suggests that the perception is entirely wiped out. [pp. 153–154]

Later in Chapter 8 of the *Outline of Psycho-Analysis*, Freud (1940a) distinguishes between the use of repression as a defense against internal instinctual demands and disavowal, perceived as a defense against the claims of the external world and linked with the concept of "splitting of the ego," castration complex, and fetishism, as we have just seen them. This initial attempt, however, was the limit of Freud's investigation of the differences between splitting and repression.

Of the post-Freudians, Melanie Klein and followers have used splitting in the same way that Freud used repression, that is, the paradigm of all defenses, the mechanism par excellence that not only determines how the mind works but also appears much earlier than repression. "Splitting," says Hanna Segal (1964) referring to Klein's contributions,

> is also the basis for what later becomes repression. If early splitting has been excessive and rigid, later repression is likely to be of an excessive neurotic rigidity. When early splitting has been less severe, repression will be less crippling, and the unconscious will remain in better communication with the conscious mind. So splitting, provided it is not excessive and does not lead to rigidity, is an extremely important mechanism of defence which not only lays the foundations for later and less primitive mechanisms, like repression, but continues to function in a modified form throughout life. [pp. 35–36]

Fairbairn (1952) does not discriminate between the two mechanisms, arguing that any discrepancy is based more on historical circumstances than on theory:

> Splitting of the ego . . . constitutes essentially the same phenomenon considered from different points of view. Here it is apposite to recall that, whilst the concept of splitting of the ego was formulated by Bleuler in an attempt to explain the phenomenon of what was known as "dementia praecox" until he introduced the term "schizophrenia" to take its place, the concept of repression was formulated by Freud in an attempt to explain the phenomenon of hysteria. [pp. 108–109]

Bion (1957) states that splitting represents the mechanism of defense chosen by the psychotic personality, or by the "psychotic part of the personality," while repression forms the most common defense among the nonpsychotic part of the personality. He says:

> The psychotic personality or part of the personality has used splitting and projective identification as a substitute for repression. Where the non-psychotic part of the personality resorts to repression as a means of cutting off certain trends in the mind both from consciousness and from other forms of manifestation and activity, the psychotic part of the personality has attempted to rid itself of the apparatus on which the psyche depends to carry out repression. [p. 52]

Using a topographical model to introduce a very interesting distinction between splitting and repression, Heinz Kohut (1971) proposes the notion of vertical as well as horizontal splitting, equating repression with the first and splitting proper with the latter. He states:

> Correlated to the last-named mechanism (i.e., disavowal) is a specific, chronic structural change to which I would like to refer, in a modification of Freud's terminology as a *vertical split in the psyche*. The ideational and emotional manifestations of a vertical split in the psyche—in contrast to such *horizontal splits* as those brought about on a deeper level by repression and on a higher level by negation—are correlated to the side-by-side, conscious existence of otherwise incompatible psychological attitudes *in depth*. [pp. 176–177]

This distinction between vertical and horizontal splitting seems to me to be of great clinical significance, and I would like to illustrate with a case what I understand Kohut to mean. For purposes of simplicity, I leave out the central argument about narcissistic structures and concentrate only on the concepts of splitting and repression.

Luis was a 36-year-old engineer, married with one child, who came to analysis because of chronic and unspecific attacks of anxiety. He was the oldest of four siblings and the only son, and had been working since he left the university, administering a factory that belonged to his very wealthy father. For the two years previous to his consultation he had been involved in an extramarital affair with a married woman who was the director of personnel in his company. He felt that he no longer loved his wife and wanted to get a divorce; however, the idea of leaving his son was very frightening and almost unbearable. He disliked his wife to the point of continually mistreating her; although she was young and good looking, he did not feel very attracted to her, and they had had no sexual relations for over a year. This condition contrasted with his relationship with his lover, whom he found very sexy and arousing. He met her about three times a week in an apartment he rented for that purpose. His only difficulty was the very strong feelings of jealousy he experienced toward her husband.

He described his mother as a very unpredictable, emotional, and inconsistent person, who always, like everybody else in his house, including himself, felt very dependent on his father, portrayed as a very powerful and domineering person. As the analysis progressed, it became clearer to him that the double life he was living (sharing nights and weekends reluctantly with his wife, while enjoying week days in the company of his lover) was the main cause of his anxiety. He also realized that this way of life was not accidental but a consequence of certain unconscious traits traceable to his childhood. Transference and countertransference were dominated by the existence of a very "dependent aspect" of the self, which outlined the content of the main projective identification. This dependent aspect had the purpose of continually inducing (countertransference) the narcissistic need to be looked after like a helpless baby. There was the incessant danger of a transferential collusion, as he did not tolerate a prolonged silence and would often ask direct questions, becoming anxious and angry when not answered, turning his head toward the analyst or sitting up on the couch. Interpretations at this time hinged on the need to show how his mind was controlled by an aspect of the self that convinced him that he was a fool, a helpless and angry little baby who needed someone else to look after him; a part of him wished to be treated like an ignorant fool, just as his father had treated him, and he felt very angry when I refused to do the same. This awareness helped him to reconstruct early memories about his relationship with his "adolescent" mother: the feeling that her dramatic mood fluctuations made her a very inconsistent person; that she gave herself with great passion toward him, as if he were her "doll," and then, perhaps out of fear, turned toward his father as a symbol of her own father and neglected Luis completely in the process.

The Oedipus complex was organized around a division in two different parts of a maternal object, kept apart by means of a vertical splitting, and representing his two dissimilar relationships with his mother (see Table 2–1). One part object (A) symbolized his narcissistic interaction with the rejecting mother—now changed into a rejected one—represented in his legal but sexless relationship with a mistreated wife, with whom he had a child and whom he could not divorce. Another part object (B) represented the idealized passionately loving mother, depicted in the passionate and illegal relationship with his girlfriend, where sex was very significant and was often performed. She was also married and he felt very jealous of her husband. Each one of these part objects, A and B, contained also a hidden and uncon-

41

Table 2–1 Organization of Positive Oedipus Relationship
(Vertical and Horizontal Splitting)

Part Object A		Part Object B
(Conscious) Legal marriage. Mistreatment of his wife. Fear of abandoning his son. Sex not performed.	V E R T I	(Conscious) Ideal relationship with a married woman. Sex is often performed. Jealous of her husband.
(Unconscious) HORIZONTAL SPLITTING or Repression	C A L	(Unconscious) HORIZONTAL SPLITTING or Repression
Repressed idea: "Rejecting mother" = legal wife of his father = his wife Repressed affect: Object split off by means of vertical splitting in three part objects: "rejecting mother," projected in his wife; impotent rejected child projected in his son; sadistic and rejecting father introjected in order to deal with castration anxiety	S P L I T T I N G	Repressed idea: "Passionate mother" = his mistress = ideal and incestuous relation with his mother behind his father's back Repressed affect: Object split by means of vertical splitting in two objects: "Passionate mother" projected in his mistress; deceived father projected in her husband

scious aspect of the positive side of his Oedipus complex, kept away from consciousness by means of repression or horizontal splitting. The "idea" repressed in part object A represents the rejecting mother and legal wife of his father, whereas the repressed "affect" pictures his anger and need for revenge against this rejecting mother by means of a sadistic interaction with his wife, as well as a fear of incest. The child portrays a part of himself he fears to abandon and the desire to secure the affect his rejecting mother had denied him in his childhood, while at the same time taking the place of his father as the head of his family. The repressed "idea" of part object B, on the other hand, depicts the illegal relationship with the passionate mother, where the split "affect" constitutes the hidden and incestuous conspiracy with the mother, and the revenge against the powerful father, now portrayed by the deceived girlfriend's husband. This figure describes only the positive aspects of the Oedipus complex; the negative features are still repressed and will constitute a deeper and (horizontal split) unconscious layer that we have not reached yet in his analysis.

Although Kohut's comparison is useful from the vantages of topography and economy, he does not explain why horizontal and vertical splitting takes place, what dynamics are involved in these different forms of defense, or what directs the ego to use one mechanism over the other. These questions might be better answered using object relations theory.

SPLITTING AFTER FREUD: OBJECT RELATIONS THEORY

From birth on there is a normal and progressive movement in cognitive integration vis-à-vis affective development, which is reflected also in the integration of emotional processes. Psychic trauma, as described by Freud and many other analysts afterward, interferes with normal emotional and cognitive processes, manufacturing within the mind an enclosed and active world described by Klein as the schizoid-paranoid position, determined by all the complicated mechanisms that go with it. According to Grotstein (1986):

> There is sufficient evidence to suggest that the infant's mode of thinking is animistic, magical, solipsistic, and personified. "Thoughts" are people or phantoms prancing around about an inner stage. The thought known as "hunger" can be the phenomenon of being stalked by a malevolent predator from within—the greedy breast, for example. Thoughts originate, in other words, as personification or, if I may modify Alfred North Whitehead, thoughts create themselves, as personified objects. "Thinking" consists of arranging objects as pawns of circumstance on some imaginary chessboard in the mind. [p. 91]

There are at least five important differences between classical theory (CT), and object relations theory (ORT): (1) the quality and nature of internal representations; (2) The importance of death instinct in the form of envy; (3) metapsychology of affect; (4) narcissism, and (5) early part-object relationships. I will deal with the first of these differences now, and leave for later some of the other considerations.

Internal Representations

The main difference between CT and ORT is that CT perceives the instinct as a permanent, object-free energy, capable of establishing object cathexis at a given moment, or giving it up accordingly, while ORT establishes that object and instinct cannot be separated. Internally the object is just a corollary of the instinct, that is, like the soul, an instinct cannot achieve a representation by itself alone, but requires the object's substance in order to acquire a presence. This different conception between CT and ORT might help us to understand the historical confusion between splitting and repression, since *it is impossible to conceive a pathological splitting that is not also repressed.* I think that it was simpler for Freud to think in terms of repression of the instinct—instead of splitting—because the instinct was conceived as pure energy, whereas for Klein, who dealt with objects rather than drives, it was easier to think in terms of splitting instead of repression. It was easier to conceive a repressed rather than split energy (instinct), or a split rather than repressed object.[2] Such a contrast, however, was not completely foreign to Freud, and this is why, I think, he tried in 1927 to institute a difference between "disavowal or splitting of the idea, and repression of the affect" (p. 22). Fairbairn (1952) had elaborated also, particularly about this last subject:

> Repression, is primarily exercised, not against impulses which have come to appear painful or "bad" (as in Freud's final view) or even against painful memories (as in Freud's earlier view), but against *internalized objects* which have come to be treated as bad, . . . also against parts of the "ego" which seek relation-

---

[2]Often, a conceptualization could be reached just from a simple detail, instead of a complex and sophisticated mental elaboration. It is said, for instance, that the word *metaphysic* had a casual origin, apparently created by Aristotle, referring to those books in his library located in the shelves *metá tá physiká.* i.e., "beyond the books of physics."

ships with these objects. . . . I had already become very much impressed by delimitations of "impulse psychology" in general, and somewhat skeptical of the explanatory value of all theories of instinct in which the instincts are treated as existing *per se.* [pp. 89–90]

On the other hand, it might be argued that splitting and repression are very well interconnected mechanisms because it is impossible to conceive part-object and part-ego structures as components of a pathological paranoid-schizoid position if they are not also repressed from consciousness. To reach consciousness, these part-object interactions must change toward integration, toward a single universe, instead of remaining divided; in other words, making the unconscious conscious automatically implies integration. This concept was also familiar to Klein's thinking in 1952:

> The mechanism of splitting underlies repression, but in contrast to the earliest form of splitting which leads to states of disintegration, repression does not normally result in a disintegration of the self. Since at this stage there is greater integration, both within the conscious and the unconscious parts to the mind, and since in repression the splitting predominantly effects a division between conscious and unconscious, neither part of the self is exposed to the degree of disintegration which may arise in previous stages. [p. 292]

NORMAL AND PATHOLOGICAL SPLITTING

Grotstein defined splitting as "the activity by which the ego discerns differences within the self and its objects, or between itself and objects." He further stated, "The ego can also split the internal perception of the relationship of objects to one another, or can experience the self as being split or fragmented by a force believed to be either within or beyond the self." (p. 3).

There are different forms of splitting: macro- and microscopic splitting; normal, that is, conscious or cognitive splitting; as well as defensive, unconscious, or pathological splitting. Klein (1946) referred to a splitting of space, epitomized by projective and introjective identification, and mentioned also Scott's suggestion about splitting of time. She stated in a footnote:

> Dr. W. C. M. Scott referred to another aspect of splitting. He stressed the importance of the breaks in the continuity of experiences, which imply a splitting in time rather than space. He referred as an instance to the alternation between states of being asleep and states of being awake. I fully agree with this point of view. [p. 6]

Macroscopic splitting usually belongs more to the realm of clinical phenomenology, equated with "dissociation," neurosis, or a "neurotic part of the personality," as explained by Bion (1967). Microscopic splitting of the mind, on the other hand, has been the concern of psychoanalytical metapsychology, initially emphasized by Klein and later on by Bion (1958), who pushed it to the extreme dimension of "particles." But he discriminates between "dissociative states" as seen in hysteria and the splitting observed in psychotics:

> The original splitting processes evinced by this patient were violent, intended to produce minute fragmenta-

tion and deliberately aimed at effecting separations which run directly counter to any natural lines of demarcation between one part of the psyche, or one function of the psyche, and another. Dissociation on the other hand appears to be gentler and to have respect for natural lines of demarcation between whole objects and indeed to follow those lines of demarcation to effect the separation; the patient who dissociates is capable of depression. [p. 69]

Cognitive splitting is normal in children's thinking or among adults, as seen for instance in religious beliefs. At the beginning of life, the world is cognitively divided, split in different areas that cannot be placed together until there is enough ego structure to conceive a total universe (object constancy); at the same time, however, the baby is dealing with a series of emotional experiences that will either ease or hinder ("continent or incontinent mother," according to Bion) the path toward integration. Cognitive splitting runs parallel with the emotional splitting I have just described. It represents how the ego envisions the world at a very early stage of development, since at that stage it is impossible to achieve a vision of the whole object, well illustrated in many of Piaget's experiments. He observed, for instance, how one of his daughters at the age of 13 months used the expression "tch tch"—a sound that designated a train she saw from the window—to name anything that moved and that she could see from that same position, whether it was a person, a horse, or the train itself. A similar behavior was observed when, instead of the window, she associated a balcony with the expression "guau-guau" to designate a dog. Just as in the previous example, the concept slid in such a way that equally under the same "sound" different objects were associated just because they were observed from the same perspective. In other words, the object's identity is not decided by its own qualities but by the capricious and particular scenario from which it has been observed. In a similar fashion, Piaget (1961) discovered that the same child used the term *panana* not only to name her grandfather, "the one who pleases her most," but anything that gave her pleasure (pp. 298–299). This cognitive splitting is a direct consequence of an early ego incapacity to integrate, but is also used to cast away emotions that might threaten identifications considered vital by the ego. Kernberg (1975) has expressed a similar view:

> Later on, what originally was a lack of integrative capacity is used defensively by the emerging ego in order to prevent the generalization of anxiety and to protect the ego core built around positive introjection (introjection and identifications established under the influence of libidinal drive derivatives). This defensive division of the ego, in which what was at first a simple defect in integration is then used actively for other purposes, is in essence the mechanism of splitting. [pp. 25–26]

Early traumatic experiences produce fixations on these kinds of primitive split or part-object relationships, creating a narcissistic structure, organized—depending on the intensity of the trauma—along the lines of either a flexible, normal splitting or a rigid and pathological schizoid-paranoid position. In narcissistic personalities, for instance, the rigid organization of this position will oppose any attempt toward depressive (depressive position) integration. Splitting, then, bring us very close to the concept of trauma and to those theoretical formulations stated by Klein, Bion, and Winnicott, among many other researchers in this field. Klein elaborated the existence of four different split objects. Of these, two are normal: "good" and "bad breast"; and two are pathological: "good idealized" and "bad persecutory". Of these four, only one is real: the good breast; the other three are only defensive ghosts. The internal representation of the good breast is made out from the experience with a satisfying, present, and real object, while the bad breast is determined by the "nontraumatic" absence of the good breast. This notion of the good breast is a complicated theoretical construct, which Bion (1957) referred to as the "continent mother," capable of "metabolizing" the raw anxiety presented by her child by means of an ego ability he called the "reverie" function.

Another aspect to consider is Bion's (1959) contribution to the concept of "attack on linking" as characteristic of the psychotic part of the personality. Referring to one of his patients, he stated:

> The extreme degree to which he has carried the splitting of objects and ego alike makes any attempt at synthesis hazardous. Furthermore, as he has rid himself of that-which-joins, his capacity for articulation, the methods available for synthesis are felt to be macilent; he can compress but cannot join, he can fuse but cannot articulate. [p. 52]

Bion (1963) also referred to a "static" form of splitting to describe the extreme stubbornness of some patients who unconsciously stick to their personal theories or delusions, regardless of what the therapist (or anybody else) might say or what a sensible logic might dictate; they will unconsciously use anything that is expressed, although it could be contradictory, to support their theories, instead of questioning them. Bion described this phenomenon as a "reversible perspective," using as an illustration the well-known silhouette of two vases standing side by side that can also be seen as two profiles facing each other. While the analyst might be talking about the vases, the patient could be thinking about the profiles or vice versa, without either realizing the discrepancy. A variant of this phenomenon is observable in some borderline patients, who at times appear to have significant insight into their situation, may even repeat what the analyst has said, but at the next session or even later in the same session appear, surprisingly, to have understood nothing at all. I call this situation the "plasticized interpretation," because the patient appears to split the apparent "insight" as if to cover it or isolate it, and then puts it aside like a foreign body or makes it disappear.

Meltzer and colleagues (1975) describe a concept called "dismantling," a defense mechanism of autistic children they differentiate from the process of splitting because of the passivity present in the traumatic experience of autism:

> We wish to envisage a structure, the ego-id-super-ego-ideal, being dismantled in a manner that has the following qualities: it must be accomplished in a moment; it must be reversible almost effortlessly, as if drawn once more together by the inertia of mental springs; its transactions must be of a quality which disqualifies them from linkage with other mental events. . . . How does this take place? We have em-

ployed the term *"dismantling,"* to which we must now give precise significance in order to differentiate it from *splitting processes*. These latter processes are understood to employ destructive impulses in order to make attacks on linking. These attacks are, in the main, directed primarily against objects, and have only a secondary consequence of splitting the ego, or, more correctly, the self. . . . We envisage "dismantling" as a very different sort of process with very different implications. In the first place it seems to us to occur in a passive rather than an active way, somewhat akin to allowing a brick wall to fall to pieces by the action of weather, moss, fungi and insects, through failing to point it with mortar . . . it would seem quite certain that neither persecutory anxiety nor despair would result from this mode of withdrawal from the world, since violence to neither self nor object is involved. [pp. 11–13]

SPLITTING OF TIME

I believe that splitting of space, as seen, for instance, in mechanisms of projective and introjective identification, appears to be a concept more common than splitting of time, although the latter is a determinant in the phenomenology of transference, where the emotional connotation attached to certain repressed events has subtracted its time, or the possibility of evolving, making them instead static and ready as a consequence for transference material only.

But there are other circumstances besides transference, or normal alteration of continuity between states of sleep and of being awake. I am thinking of a psychotic patient who became ill just after his younger brother committed suicide at the age of 22. The main problem I faced with this patient, as is usually the case with psychotics, was difficulty in following the bizarre stream of associations that outlined his speech. It became clear afterward that he was very attached to his brother. When they were 11 and 13, respectively, the patient shot his brother accidentally with a homemade gun; although the brother very nearly died, he recovered completely. Then I discovered that the apparent incomprehension of the manifest content of my patient's speech was the consequence of some kind of monologue: he would utter a word as expressing a desire, then immediately would express another word in anticipation of what he thought I would say. Apparently he was trapped between two different moments of his life: the present, when his brother had killed himself, and the past, when he shot the brother. He appeared to be saying, under extreme pressure and with great speed: "I shot my brother, but he didn't die, but he is dead, but he shot himself, but I shot him, but he didn't die," and so on. It was his only way of dealing with the unbearable burden imposed by the threats of a sadistic superego, owing to guilt about his own fratricidal impulses, now exercised in the transference.

SPLITTING AND INTEGRATION

In discussing his concept of a "holding environment," Winnicott (1960b) stated: "It will be seen, therefore, that the work of Klein on the splitting defence mechanisms and on projections and so on, is an attempt to state the effects of failure of environmental provision in terms of the individual" (p. 50). Early ego splitting, cognitive as well as emotional, requires the presence of a special capacity provided by the environment that will equip the primitive ego with the faculty to reduce the process of defensive splitting (separating good from bad) and enhance normal integrative mastery. I think that such a faculty, usually supplied by the mother, may be defined, regardless of the name we give to it, *as the capacity to provide an environment that will, harmonically and progressively, extend the maturational disposition sustained by the uterus.* Several psychoanalysts have researched this particular field and have described various "objects" and "functions" responsible for the structuring of such inner integrative capacity. I am thinking of Klein's good breast, Winnicott's "holding" or "good-enough mother," Bion's reverie function, and more recently, Grotstein's "background object of primary identifications." "In my terminology" says Winnicott (1960a), "the good-enough mother is able to meet the needs of her infant at the beginning, and to meet these needs so well that the infant, as emergence from the matrix of the infant–mother relationship takes place, is able to have a brief *experience of omnipotence*" (p. 57). Grotstein (1986), on the other hand, declares: "The experience of being in splits is mitigated by the experience of at-one-ment or self-cohesiveness which, in the language of experience, is achieved by actions emanating from the presence of the phantasy of what I call the *Background Object of Primary Identification*" (p. 77).

Although I am aware that the main purpose of his description is to emphasizes the "background" and "holding" qualities of the experience, we could also infer, from the description of his patients, that this background object seem to relate as well to the father's penis: "Several of the patients were able either to dream or to phantasy that they

54

wished to have a *highly idealized object behind them on whose lap they could sit and whose power they could feel, but they would not have to be aware of the importance of this object face-to-face*" (p. 80; italics mine).

Grotstein also refers to the patient with a recurrent nightmare, a *plain and smooth surface* that changed into a *wrinkled one*. This observation is important because it introduces the relevance of the penis, besides the breast, as an integrative object that continues the differentiation established by the mother. We might conceive thus of the "good-enough father," since it is the father who breaks the symbiotic and narcissistic relationship with the mother and introduces the triangulation of the Oedipus complex; in other words, the phallus, like a wedge, cleaves the narcissistic fusion of self and object by introducing the symbol. Many will argue, however, that oedipal space is mostly possible because it is previously present within the mother's unconscious fantasy; otherwise, the inclusion of the father role and the creation of the Oedipus triangulation could not be achieved. Often we find in our clinical practice that delinquent and perverted behaviors show an important fault in the role of the father, either total absence or an "incontinent" attitude (López-Corvo 1993).

NOTHINGNESS AND OTHERNESS

False Self and True Self, or the Inversion of the Natural Order of Desire

An important form of splitting was pointed out by Winnicott (1960a) when he referred to "false and true self," a condition often seen in certain borderline patients: "In one case, a man patient who had had a considerable amount of analysis before coming to me, my work really started with him when I made clear to him that I recognized his non-existence. . . . When I said that . . . he felt that he had been communicated with for the first time" (pp. 140–152). The main characteristic of this kind of patient is the existence of a facade, or thousands of facades, I should say, that are continually presented to others, regardless of who these persons might be, although strongly influenced by idealization or by projection of idealized objects. This facade, or false self, represents an attitude the patient dispenses to the Other, a defense against castration anxiety, attempting to deceive potential castrators, controlling them by providing a false posture as compliance. The false self depicts a specific image the patient feels, they—the others—want him or her to be. In the same vein there is the opposite reaction, seen in most acting out, where the patient decides to provide to others exactly the opposite of what he or she feels others want him or her to be. Both conditions, either pleasing via a "positive identification," or attacking by means of a "negative" one, are simply different sides of the same coin, meaning that both behaviors are completely conditioned by the Other's desire. In other words, there is an inversion of the natural order of the desire, where the Other's desire is always placed before the person's desire.

A 29-year-old drug addict had managed to control his habit for the previous two years. Following a hiatus for holidays, he relapsed into drinking with friends and later, when very intoxicated, abandoned the group in order to procure cocaine in a highly dangerous red-light district.

The next morning he found himself wandering with two complete strangers on a distant and isolated beach, with no recollection whatsoever about what had happened. When he recounted these events, he appeared extremely upset, describing the facts with great difficulty, and feeling very embarrassed and guilty about what happened. He felt terrible when confronted by his father, puzzled about how he could have so disappointed him, as well as his girlfriend, certain that he was a complete failure, that he had done terrible damage to everybody, including the therapy, and so on. He went on during the whole hour apologizing to everyone, including me. But he never mentioned the tremendous risk he had taken wandering alone in the wee hours, in a very dangerous section of the city, accompanied by people he didn't even know, in such an intoxicated state that he didn't even remember what had happened. It was as if he didn't even exist, that only others were important; because, after all, he had done nothing to his parents, girlfriend, or analyst by taking one day off from work, drinking, and taking drugs. The real problem was the danger he had placed himself in. He was lucky that nothing really happened to him. His personality split into at least three elements: (1) a *pleasing aspect*, (2) a *negativistic, acting out destructive aspect,* and (3) in between, the *true self* he was trying to develop. The pleasing element was a form of keeping the others alive (parents, girlfriend, and analyst), giving to them exactly what he thought they all wanted from him. Such a confused commitment would also induce strong feelings of envy and anger against those he felt forced to please and comply with, as well a desire to attack and destroy them through acting out (the destructive element) whatever idealized object he had projected in them. Afterward appeared the persecution for the "crime" he felt he had committed against the others, followed by the need to comply again and then to attack, in an endless vicious cycle. At the end, however, his true self was hopelessly trapped between the pleasing and destructive elements, and the purpose of the treatment at this point, was to help him uncover and reconstruct his true self. Or as another patient, having insight about this situation, said paraphrasing Proust: "Je suis à la recherche de mon désir perdu."

In this case we observe the existence of two different kinds of analytical couples. On the one hand there is the demanding analyst with the pleasing patient, giving the impression of an impeccable analysis: the perfect analyst and the perfect patient. At the same time there is a hidden couple, integrated by the negative-envious patient and the envied and denigrated analyst, where transference–countertransference interactions occur, similar to a negative therapeutic reaction: acting out carries the purpose of attacking the analyst by destroying the "perfect" patient.

Iatrogenic Splitting

Since the publication of *The Three Faces of Eve* (Thigpen and Cleckley 1958), it has been common to see therapists introducing patients who display, not just three faces but as many as twenty or more—a kind of competition for a greater number of personalities with different names, dissimilar postures and all. I have often thought that such conditions represent a perverse relationship between these therapists and their borderline patients, who, via projective identification of exhibitionist tendencies, induce in the therapists a need to act out, countertransferentially, their voyeuristic counterpart, generating a sort of vicious cycle or perverse collusion: the greater the interest of the therapist in the patient's dissociation, the greater the number of "personalities" the patient will happily provide for the therapist, the greater the interest of the therapist, and so forth.

3

Defensive Splitting and Schizoid Phenomena

THE SCHIZOID PHENOMENA

A number of intimate mechanisms are responsible for the appearance and increment of pathological splitting mechanisms, which, according to Bion (1957), are more common among psychotics and seriously character disordered or borderline cases, that is, the "psychotic aspect of the personality." Some of these cases have been studied by other researchers in the field of psychoanalysis and from differing clinical perspectives, such as Deutsch's "as if," Betty Joseph's "difficult patients," Winnicott's "false self," Rosenfeld's "destructive narcissism," or Meltzer's "pseudo-adults." In fact, all of these patients could be

Note. A version of this chapter was previously published in *Melanie Klein and Object Relations,* 11: 1–94, 1993, and is reprinted by permission of The Ontario Institute for Studies in Education.

classified as borderline or narcissistic personalities whose main features are related to the "schizoid phenomena" as described by Klein (1946), Fairbairn (1952), and later by Guntrip (1969). Other authors such as Meltzer (1966) and more recently Tustin (1972) have matched the same pathology to findings observed in autistic children.

Splitting and projection appear as very primitive mechanisms exercised by the ego in order to rid itself of any unpleasant experience. The necessary environmental requirements capable of guaranteeing sufficient protection to the baby constitute such a complex intermingling of variables that Winnicott (1960a) and Bion (1957), among many others, both developed a generalized concept to define this intricate equilibrium: the good-enough mother and the continent mother, respectively. As previously mentioned, when the intrauterine mother–baby interaction is not continued and maintained after birth in a manner compatible with those conditions described by Winnicott and Bion, split mechanisms, as well as projection, will increase accordingly, and as an aftermath a serious disruption in the development of magic-omnipotent defense mechanisms may occur. Klein (1946), however, has made a strong point about the interaction between inner and outer realities; that is, regardless of the threatening qualities of the environment, there also exist substantial inner feelings of anger and an inherited aggressive drive or death instinct that will always interplay with the environment. Even if the mother meant well, the children might react on their own with aggression. Guntrip (1969) stated:

> The ego splits itself because of its fear of its own death instinct, without and prior to any relationship with objects; the badness of the object is determined, not by experience of the object, but by projection of the death

64

> instinct, and the badness of the self is felt, not in
> relation to objects, but because it is in part constituted
> by a death instinct. Everything begins with the ego's
> fear of its own death instinct. [p. 414]

The relation between the baby and the breast is used
by Klein as a paradigm of all early interactions. Proper
satisfaction of hunger represents the good breast, whereas
hunger and absence of the breast represents the bad breast.
A balance between these two conditions guarantees the
future possibility of a low level of suffering; after all, a non-
life-threatening absence of the breast induces a healthy
anger, the necessity to phantasize that absence in order to
recreate the lost object, as well as the need for creativity,
and later on, the need to *name* the absent object—in other
words, creative thinking and speech. It constitutes Klein's
"normal schizo-paranoid position," formed only by two
part objects: good and bad breast. A prolonged life-threatening absence of the breast, on the other hand, will induce
a high level of annihilatory anxiety, or panic, provoking the
need to split off such a threat and to project it outside to the
external object. Anger, envy, need for omnipotent control of
the object, and persecutory anxiety are feelings that will
also increase accordingly with the intensity of the threat.
These mechanisms constitute the dynamic of the schizoid
phenomena, or more specifically, Klein's "pathological
schizo-paranoid position," formed by four objects: the bad
and good objects, as well as the good idealized and the bad
persecutory ones. It is the intensity of a minute splitting,
together with an extreme rigidity, that distinguishes this
pathological position from a normal one.

Several clinical consequences reflect the transference–
countertransference dimension. Guntrip (1969), for instance, has emphasized the presence of strong feelings of

ambivalence as an important characteristic of the "schizoid condition." He states:

> You are always *impelled* into a relationship by your needs and at once *driven out* again by fear either of exhausting your love-object by the demands you want to make or else losing your own individuality by over-dependence and identification. This "in and out" oscillation is the *typical schizoid behavior*, and to escape from it into detachment and loss of feeling is the *typical schizoid state*. [p. 48]

Other characteristics are a sensation of depersonalization or derealization; a feeling of no identity, of ego emptiness; a fear of ego collapse; inhibition of the capacity to love or to relate to other persons; and a fear of sleep or relaxation.

Besides difficulties related to the complexity of circumstances and characteristics of psychic trauma, questions of cross-cultural differences arise between observations described by the authors I have mentioned above, derived from work with Anglo-Saxon patients, and the observations I gathered while working with Latinos. Because autism, now in fashion, seems to be related more to obsessive traits as observed in Anglo-Saxons, I prefer the use of a more general term, such as *schizoid phenomena*.

QUANTITATIVE (DEPRESSION) AND QUALITATIVE (SCHIZOID PHENOMENA) ASPECTS OF DISTURBED MOTHER–CHILD NATURAL SYMBIOSIS

Differences between depression and schizoid phenomena appear to be closely related to the characteristics of disturbances taking place during the mother–child natural symbiosis, a phenomenology so well described through the years by so many researchers that I will not repeat it: Ferenczi (1933), Deutsch (1937), A. Freud and Burlingham (1944), Bowlby (1960), Greenacre (1960, 1968), Steel and Pollock (1968), Shengold (1979), and so on. I will add only, that prolonged absence of the mother (quantitative) during this early period of life usually results later on in clinical features of anxious and depressive disorders, while disturbances related more to the quality of the relationship, the presence–absence type of conflict, are more responsible for schizoid reactions.

Guntrip (1969) discriminated between depressive and schizoid phenomena in this manner:

> Complaints of feeling cut off, shut off, out of touch, feeling apart or strange, of things being out of focus or unreal, of not feeling one with people, or of the point having gone out of life, interest flagging, things seeming futile and meaningless, all describe in various ways this state of mind. Patients usually call it "depression," but it lacks the heavy, black, inner sense of brooding, of anger and guilt, which are not difficult to discover in classic depression. Depression is really a more extroverted state of mind, which, while the patient is turning his aggression inward against himself, is part of a struggle not to break out into overt angry and aggressive behavior. The states described above are rather the "schizoid states." They are definitely introverted. Depression is object-relational. The schizoid person has renounced objects, even though he still needs them. . . . The schizoid condition consists in the first place in an attempt to cancel external object-relations and live in a detached and withdrawn way. [pp. 17–18]

MOTHERS' CULTURAL BACKGROUND AND SCHIZOID PHENOMENA: PREDOMINANCE OF OBSESSIVE DEFENSES IN ANGLO-SAXON MOTHERS AND PHOBIC (AVOIDANCE) DEFENSES IN LATINO MOTHERS

Obsessive defenses

Two aspects at least are relevant to this type of defense. One is "psychogenic autism," complying with evaluations made by Meltzer (1966) and Tustin (1972) of autistic children, as well as S. Klein (1980) of neurotic patients. The other relates to the concept of "cumulative trauma" as described by Khan (1974) following contributions from Freud (1920).

Psychogenic Autism

I have previously suggested that psychogenic autism often implies a brain-damaged child's response to the projective identification of the mother, who has withdrawn her affect by the use of obsessive defenses in order to ward off filicidal impulses induced by the narcissistic injury of having given birth to a brain-damaged child. I based this statement on clinical observations as well as family studies and empirical findings such as the comparison between "autistic psychosis" (Kanner 1944) on one hand, and "symbiotic psychosis" (Mahler 1952) on the other. I had observed its incidence in northern countries such as Canada and tropical ones such as Venezuela. While "autism" is more common in the former, the relation is inverted in the latter.

The hypothesis I then introduced was based on the ego's different forms of defense organization, used to avoid the narcissistic pain experienced by mothers unable to resolve their unconscious feelings of phallic envy. In Anglo-Saxon cultures, which generally manifest more obsessive traits than do Latino cultures, mothers very often use defense mechanisms such as reaction formation, anal retention, or passive aggression. In Latino cultures, on the other hand, where hysterical traits are more common, mechanisms of manic denial and direct and open forms of aggression are more frequent. Kanner's (1944) original description, and most of all his definition of the "refrigerator mother," used to illustrate mothers' obsessive detachment, prompted many researchers to sway to the other extreme, becoming the devil's advocate and objecting that too much responsibility was laid on the parents, who already were suffering the birth of a sick and difficult child. In any case, the fact that psychogenic autism improves with psychoanalytical psychotherapy would seem to indicate that the environment is determinant and that Kanner's original statement still holds. The exact details of how such maternal rejection takes place may be very difficult to observe, so personal, so specific is it to the mother–child relationship, that I have referred to it as the "schizoid secret."

In their investigations of autism, Meltzer and colleagues (1966) described a new defense mechanism, "different from projective identification," they said, which they called *dismantling*, a term I have previously described. Using Bion's language, dismantling will result as a consequence of the "mother's incontinence," because the *good breast* acts as cohesion, like an interstitial tissue that anchors the perspective; when this fails, *senses* will drift because they lack a "common sense" that will hold them together. Meltzer and colleagues (1966) observed: "When this (good breast) withers, as it probably does when depression or other disturbance in the mother dries up her attentiveness, warmth, chatter and sensuality toward the baby, the dismantled self will tend to float away for longer and longer periods of mindless activity" (p. 16).

However, the dismantling mechanism would appear to constitute for the child a narcissistic identification with the mother's own obsessive dismantling capacity, at least in psychogenic autism. This mechanism is the direct consequence of the mother's aggression, via anal sadistic and obsessive mechanisms, in the face of the narcissistic injury of the phallic fault; she is dissatisfied because her child was born abnormal, and the child becomes the place where she continuously projects undesired aspects of herself. The child then dismantles by virtue of the mother dismantling him or her, denying love and affection (perceptive systems) as a form of reaction formation or passive aggression. This mechanism is probably more common among mothers from northern cultures, where the defense, as an obsessive "solution," is more frequent than in Latino cultures. It is logical then to conclude, as Meltzer has done, that there is a close relation between autism and obsessive behavior.

Cumulative Trauma

Based on the phenomenon of the "protective shield" originally described by Freud (1920), Masud Khan (1974) introduced the concept of "cumulative trauma," something that could take place during that period of development when the infant needs and uses the mother as a protective shield. Events could become traumatic once that shield is broken. The mother becomes a protective shield according to a complex interaction described by Winnicott (1951) as the "good-enough mother," by Bion (1967) as the "continent-reverie," and by Hartmann (1964) as the "average expectable environment." The mother's failure in her role of protective shield induces in the infant a condition of cumulative trauma. Khan (1974) said: "In this context it would be more accurate to say that these breaches over the course of time and through the developmental process accumulate silently and invisibly" (p. 47). Although neither the moment nor the context in which the trauma has taken place appears traumatic, the trauma accumulates silently and may only be reconstructed in retrospect.

Some time ago, while working in Canada, I had the opportunity to analyze a woman who fit well Khan's description of cumulative trauma. Louise was born into a high-class, white Protestant family, in a quiet rural area near Toronto. Her parents were both professionals. The second of five children, Louise was blond, attractive, single, and looked much younger in appearance and behavior than her stated age of 32 years. It was difficult to give any sense to the intangible happenings of those apparently uneventful early years that could help us to grasp, understand, or justify the intense level of suffering that she presented at the moment of her consultation. She spoke with a low, soft voice, reflecting a mixture of naïveté and surprise, which gave her face a shy and childlike

71

expression. She complained about feeling anxious, lonely, and depressed, and was convinced that people would find out that a third generation of relatives on her father's side were European Jews. Her emotions while describing these fantasies were so intense they brought to my mind the time of the Nazi occupation of Europe or the Spanish Inquisition. Her conviction had the characteristic of an *idée fixe*, of a monosymptomatic delusion in an otherwise clear sensorium. It elicited countertransferentially, at this early stage of the analysis, the desire to engage in an explanation that would prove the absurdity of her concern. Surprisingly, however, this delusional idea gave way very soon, almost drastically, to another idea of equal emotional intensity, perhaps less ludicrous but one that lasted longer: she feared she might be a lesbian and provided facts and accounts to back her concern. She liked and felt strongly attracted to a female teacher at the university, and recalled—and recounted like a confession—a childhood experience with another classmate. At the end of the third session still during the assessment period, while we were both standing up and she was ready to leave, she surprised me by throwing her arms around me and holding me tight for a few seconds. It was not a sexual approach from a seductive woman, but I experienced instead the strong need of a desolate child, hungry and desperate for affection, a need for security provided by a holding mother. Several times after this incident she verbalized similar desires and once attempted to repeat that previous experience. This desire dissipated as we had a better opportunity to

72

analyze its significance. I felt a sense of contradiction between her pubertal appearance, her *idée fixe*, and her need for affection, and the behavior we might expect to result from a high-middle-class, well-organized environment, which showed no particular signs of deprivation and where both parents were professionals. As an analyst coming from a different culture, still in a period of adjustment when the analysis started, I was struck by my inability to identify any logical cause or to single out any determining event that might explain the level of suffering observed in this patient. In Latino culture the kind of symptomatology presented by Louise would usually be linked to significant traumatic events (death, separation, etc.) during early childhood, often tinged with hysteria, covering up the history of an early oral deprivation and fixation with facade of overt pseudo-femininity.[1]

Phobic and Avoidance Mechanisms

Phobic mechanisms are more common in Latino cultures, where overstimulation and deprivation go hand in hand in a fashion Shengold (1979), paraphrasing "Senatspräsident" Schreber, calls "soul murder." This phenomenology tallies with the mother's presence–absence condition mentioned previously, though it is different from the behavior of the mother of the autistic child, who is present but has

---

[1] I often wonder that perhaps it was not by chance that Masud Khan described this kind of pathology, but being from Pakistan he was also taken, as was I, by the differences of both cultures, Hindu and English in his case; Spanish Latino in mine.

withdrawn all her affect in a dismantling fashion: she is there, but inanimate. Phobic mothers behave differently. I have referred to the dynamic of "cataclysmic peace" to describe some families who alternate between states of great overt anxiety and periods of complete denial.

On one occasion I had the opportunity to assist, lamentably for a very short time, a young male patient addicted to intravenous cocaine for several years, whom I will call Ismael. He had a long history of drug abuse, as well as many years of treatment at home and abroad. He was the youngest of three brothers of parents who divorced when he was only 3 years old. His mother did not marry again but had a close relationship with the same person for several years, a rather shy and distant man who apparently saw in her some kind of a powerful mother image. Ismael was a good-looking, soft-spoken, intelligent, and reserved young man, whom I saw only five times before he committed suicide by overdose. His appearance contrasted with the intensity of his suffering, the feeling of being absolutely trapped and hopeless that finally brought him to his tragic end, despite his many years of treatment. I felt in the short time I saw him that any initiative, even before it could be attempted, was bound to yield to the malignant power of an internal diabolical object that enslaved his mind and induced the feeling of absolute impotence; a powerless baby totally hopeless, whose only purpose was to control a mother he felt not only as powerful and indispensable but also as intense, uncontrollable, arbitrary, and unpredictable—a situation that could be completely reversed if the mother felt frightened either by internal or external threats. When that happened, she switched completely to a helpless child in total panic, the "terror without a name," as Bion once expressed it. The narcissistic bond between the patient and his mother was so tight, so excluding and deeply defended, that any attempt to intervene was impossible. Its core was buried deep inside the self, hidden behind a facade of false self, "as if," or pseudo-maturity—impregnable. This explained, of course, why all attempts at treatment failed. This pathology appeared to overpower all Ismael's behavior: the symbiotic and ambivalent relationship with his mother, with no rescue attempt made by the absent father, a phallus capable of fracturing the narcissistic interaction and allowing the oedipal triangulation to take place. In this sense, Ismael's suicide presented the paradox of dying in order not to continue living—forever tied to a narcissistic plot within a delusional core, whose main dynamic was a polarization between a powerless baby felt inside and an omnipotent mother projected outside. The real danger appeared when the mother, playing the role of the powerful-omnipotent mother, suddenly turned the tables and became—arbitrarily and unpredictably—the powerless baby, forcing her unprepared son to become the powerful mother. Whenever this change took place, it filled the patient with an intense and paralyzing panic; he was caught in a trap he could neither act out (the omnipotent mother) nor escape.

I also saw the mother for a short time after the boy's death. Although we did not have much of a chance to observe her unconscious phantasies, some aspects were so obvious that it was easy to deduce them. For instance, the drama she brought to any statement: gesture overpowering content, usually ending the conversation with some kind of pompous conceit, moving her hands for emphasis while throwing her loose hair back, accompanied by two or three short intakes of breath, her face red and bloated, appearing intensely burdened. Her statements bespoke imminent transcendence, absolute and total necessity barring any other possibility: "It was that and nothing else." But then, in great contrast to the atmosphere of seriousness and impending danger she had just managed to create, and after a brief silence, she would turn with a childish and frightened countenance, guilty and uncertain, to obtain approval from her husband, who, up to this moment, had sat quietly looking at the floor, giving an impression of inattentive endorsement. Her last gesture reminded me of the notion of "refilling," exhibited by babies toward their mothers during the phase of "rapprochement" described by Mahler (1972a), p. 119; 1972b, p. 131). The intensity of her account, the feeling of "knowing all," of being the only source of truth, and so forth, completely belied her look of scolded child, who in the end searched for approval in her husband's passive acknowledgment and usually responded under the pressure of a powerful projective identification. Notes I wrote at the time describing the events read as follows:

> Certain actions take place or are instrumented with
> intense vehemence and then left aside with pretension

and paralyzing disdain, with the main purpose of overwhelming the object by compromise, while at the same time also paralyzing, because it becomes impossible to predict what might come next. She is [the mother] a little girl staggered by the weight of an internal object that forces her to make gestures heavy with emptiness. The "action" takes place impulsively, not as a result of inductive or deductive elaborations, but by contiguity, capriciously associated by cathexis, by conspicuous features, with the purpose of trying an idea or a fact that she presupposes as true. The "truth" is not achieved by deduction but by tyranny, imposed from above, by caprice, determined by an arbitrary and unpredictable private truth, useful as a material to build intrusive projective identifications. It corresponds, I think, to Bion's bizarre objects.

There is also among these patients a history of incidents, sometimes unmentioned in their narration, but obvious in the level of suffering and specific characteristics of the transference and countertransference, such as early maternal separation, postpartum depression, death, and so forth.

I remember the case of a young woman—I will call her Nydia—single, initially forced by her father to look for help because of marijuana and cocaine addiction, and capable of keeping up of her own accord with daily sessions for around six months, until just after the first summer holidays, when she refused to continue, changing the initial positive transference to a complete rejection of the analyst. She was the youngest and only girl of three siblings, her older brothers being rather successful professionals, married and apparently well

77

adjusted. An older daughter was stillborn, an event that had significant and fatalistic consequences for Nydia, because something similar had also happened to her mother, whose sister—Nydia's aunt—died shortly after birth from malaria soon after her parents—Nydia's grandparents—had emigrated from Chile. Unresolved mourning induced by displacement Nydia's identification not only with her dead sister but also with her dead aunt: she was both her grandparents' daughter and granddaughter, and her mother's sister and daughter; not to mention that on her father side she was the first girl in two generations. The enormous weight of so many sufferings and broken expectations had induced in Nydia the need to shelter herself under the cover of Winnicott's false self or Deutsch's "as if" personality structure. She was the fetish toy of two generations, continuously exposed to the ambivalent inconsistencies of certain kinds of object relations that filled her with all and nothingness, with life and death, with hope and frustration: hope because she was the unconscious depository of several family ghosts, and frustration, because at the same time she was not. She had a "delusional" belief that she was the "president," "manager," or "vice president," and so on, of several of her father's companies, and she had all sort of letters and fancy visiting cards to prove it; but it was all nominal. Just as in a child's game, she only played at it, giving the transference impression of the "princess–beggar": she had all and nothing; she was the manic denial of death, the delusional ghost of both her aunt and sister, but at the same time, death itself. Analysis was also some kind of children's game, where

I, just like her father, demanded from her the condition of "analysand," something she played at with little commitment. This condition continued until the first summer holiday, when she fell in with an older cocaine addict as a defense against separation and annihilation anxiety, a transferential acting out that resulted in such rejection of any further treatment that hospitalization was then required.

The Schizoid Secret

An important aspect of the schizoid phenomena is an inability to remember early circumstances surrounding the facts. They cannot be named or made conscious spontaneously because they are not, as Bion has stated, material for thinking but instead are translated into feelings, sensations, or incomprehensible perceptions, capable of being reconstructed only secondhand. They are overall material for dreams, substance for transference and countertransference dimensions, very often detected by only these means, through the impact of intrusive and painful projective identifications. There is such a silence in the manifest content of the discourse that I have come to think of it as a "schizoid secret." Two circumstances may serve as a paradigm for revealing the "secrecy" observed in certain schizoid mechanisms. One refers to clinical observations as seen in the presence–absence type of mother–child interaction. The other situation I came across while investigating a historical-mythological event related to the Eleusinian Mysteries.[2] Presence–absence refers to the in-

---

[2]The Eleusinian Mysteries requires some explanation, but since it served as an inspiration for the concept of the schizoid

timate and silent capacity (dismantling) of the obsessive (Anglo-Saxon) mother to detach her feelings of aggression from her child as a reaction-formation and anal-sadistic kind of passive aggression, or the mental turmoil, never understood by the child, induced by the phobic (Latino) mother by means of continuous interplay of overstimulation and deprivation.

These particular characteristics of the schizoid phenomena, or the schizoid secret could also be observed in dreams or in the transference:

Elisabeth was a young woman of Hungarian background, married with two children. She requested analytical treatment because of depression and alcohol dependence. She was the older of two

---

secret, I think the explanation is worth the trouble. Such mysteries were celebrated by the ancient Greeks and Romans for more than fourteen hundred years. They represented a single night's experience for more than three thousand initiates during a supposed "trip" to the underworld to accompany the goddess Persephone as she reunited with her husband Hades every year at the beginning of winter. What exactly took place during this experience, attended over the years by well-known Greeks and Romans such as Aristotle, Demosthenes, Plato, Marcus Aurelius, and so on, was completely unknown until recently, when in the mid-1960s K. Kerenyi, a specialist in myths, discovered that the *Kykeon*, a mixture of oats and mint drunk by all the initiates during that night might also have been contaminated with ergot (LSD). The toxic and hallucinatory reaction we often see now with LSD is so private that it would have been impossible for the Greeks to share the experience among themselves, mostly because they did not possess the knowledge of its significance we have now.

siblings, although her younger brother died when she was very little. Her parents separated when she was only 3 years old, possibly, she believes, after her brother's death. Because of her mother's several occupations and need for traveling, she grew up very lonely, always in the hands of maids and governesses, without friends to play with, in a world of fantasies she referred as a parody of Milner's "rich poor child."

After eight months of analysis, five times a week, she came for a Thursday session (which I will summarize), the last one before the Christmas holidays, since I had canceled the Friday session four days before. She said: "I went to the bank to get the money to pay you, but the person who always gets me the change wasn't there, and I could not convince the other teller who was in his place to do it. I begged him, threatened, even seduced him, but to no avail. I used my husband's name: How is it possible that a Grantzidis . . . ? but I couldn't; finally I had to call my father-in-law. . . . When in my life had I ever called my father-in-law, to borrow money from him? Never; it is unbelievable how much I have changed. . . ." (long pause) In the countertransference I felt that she only wanted to say that because she didn't know what else to say, and was waiting for my answer. She continued: "And Antonio [the father-in-law] is completely crazy about Vicente [her younger child], and ordered a train from the States for his Christmas present. Now everybody is trying to put it together; it is not like before when he only gave money to Vicente . . . and he had to pay something like sixty thousand bolivars to Customs. But he convinced them that it was a company sample and finally paid only six thousand bolivars." Then I said that perhaps she felt a bit disappointed with me, because I did not behave toward her as Antonio had done with Vicente, doing everything possible to get him a present, or like herself, since she also went into complicated maneuvers to get my money before I left. Instead, I had decide to leave on holidays and to abandon her prematurely.

"I remember a dream: *I am with Vicente in his room and there is a giraffe, a beautiful wooden giraffe. Vicente goes to bed, and an older man comes inside. He is like a mad scientist—like a madman—with a box, like a food container. Inside is something horrible. It is like a piece of meat that moves by itself; it is throbbing, but only when I look at it. I point to the man that the thing is alive, but as soon as he looks at it, it stops pulsing. I am afraid because I feel he doesn't know what he is doing. And I try to leave the room, but he follows me trying to give me an injection. Then I am in another room and there is a lighted swimming pool, and they are doing experiments with monkeys, but don't know what they are doing. They take a monkey and put it in the pool, and it explodes. Then they try to experiment with cold water, and ice starts to form in the water. A man jumps inside the pool and sinks to the bottom, and I start to feel anxious. I decide to look for him and jump in the water too. But when I reach the bottom, I realize that he is just a wire dummy.*

"The giraffe was beautiful, but made only of

wood, not covered with a soft material as they usually are. The scientist could be you. The experiment with the monkeys reminds me of Harlow's movies. I don't like the smell of raw meat; it disgusts me."

Through the mechanism of a complex unconscious phantasy, the dream seems to summarize most of her conflicts: First, the memory of something "cold": a giraffe without skin and Harlow's monkeys with their surrogate mothers. At the same time a sense of distrust: the "mad scientist" and the persistent feeling that he might not know what he is doing, that all her past maternal deprivation could be repeated and she might be hurt again. It might involve also a degradation of the object in order to avoid separation anxiety: if I am not good—not knowing what I am doing—she could drop me anytime. But the greatest source of anxiety comes from not being able to share her feelings, that only she and nobody else can see the meat throbbing, just as might take place between autistic children and their obsessive mothers: the dismantling mechanism used by the mother to reject the autistic child is so private that nobody witnesses it. But it could also have another meaning, that I might not be a witness to the panic she experiences when the spoils of her parents, whom she had enviously killed and destroyed, are returned to her in the meat that she eats—a fear common among many vegetarians.

Understanding the meaning of the discourse is often not possible; it became necessary in this situation to use countertransference to elaborate the interpretation, something I have referred to as a blind interpretation or "interpreting by instruments."

For instance, Irma was a young woman, looking much younger than her stated age. Although she made some improvement, she was also increasingly resistant to keeping her daily appointments, missing between two and three sessions weekly. The situation worsened after the August holidays. We had worked on her fear of abandonment, based on an early experience she had when she was around 18 months old. Her mother was hospitalized abroad for several months, her father left on a business trip, and she had to remain with a governess who didn't speak any Spanish at all. Although she did not remember this experience very clearly, she found that several recurrent dreams reflected that reality, once her images were compared with her mother's accounts of the time of her hospitalization and the physical characteristics of the institution. Resistance to continuing treatment increased even after investigating several outlets such as separation anxiety, narcissistic rage caused by fear of abandonment during holidays, fear of losing control of the external object, fear of dependency, envy in the face of the breast's omnipotence, idealization of the bad object, and so forth. Shortly after, however, I decided to finally respond to a countertransference feeling I had being experimenting with for quite some time. It was often there, but I had neither paid attention to nor attempted to interpret it. Very regularly I had a sensual, more than sexual, sensation—more a feeling than a thought or a fantasy—very subtle and distant, which I was usually aware of only when I questioned myself about my countertransference. Although the patient was physically pleasant, I did not think she was capable of freely inducing such feelings: her childish countenance, mindless and unwomanly attitude, puerile body, and so on were not exactly physical characteristics that could explain the sensuality I often experienced. I am now referring to the possibility of using very primitive and censorial projective identifications to elaborate the interpretation, similar to those suggested by Heimann (1950), Racker (1953), Grinberg (1957, 1976), Rosenfeld (1971), and others. One day just after Irma was describing how her alcoholic father liked to fondle and kiss her when drunk, I decided to use my countertransference to interpret her resistance about making the analysis important in her life. I told her I thought she might fear that I could become like her father and try to fondle and kiss her instead of understanding the real nature of her needs, that I might confuse her mouth with her vagina, the breast with the penis. Then she talked about how frightened she felt every time her father was drunk and started to fondle her, and that she also heard stories about male psychiatrists who went to bed with their female patients. Further interpretation along these oedipal lines helped strengthen her commitment to the treatment.

Threats to the Possibility of Omnipotent Object Control

I think that the schizoid phenomenon takes place once the infant's need to maintain a continuous omnipotent object control is chronically threatened and even hindered. Usually such a threat takes place due either to complete absence of the mother or to the phenomenology of the presence–absence. Once this process takes place, several mechanisms might appear: splitting; increment of auto-erotic behavior; formation of a pathological transitional space as well as the fetish toy; idealization of the bad object, often represented by idealization of feces and their derivatives; self-envy mechanisms or any behavior unaccepted by certain aspects of the superego (negativism). Autoerotism is incremented with the purpose of obliterating the dependency on the breast, a mechanism responsible for a great amount of persecutory anxiety. Guilt from masturbation usually derives from the need to deny object dependency, to render it worthless and incompetent, because mourning for the breast during the process of weaning has not yet been achieved. An increment of omnipotent control may be observed in patients who show characteristics of what I call the "Atlas complex," a belie. that they are absolutely indispensable, an inability to delegate, a perpetual feeling of responsibility for others, such as parents and friends. Transferentially they have the feeling that they could easily manage without treatment, that they continue coming in order to "look after" the analyst, something they also resent and that sometimes not only induces a negative transference but is also responsible for interrupting the treatment if not interpreted in time. These dynamics are related to the phenomenology of "essentiality," or the need to be exceptional (Freud 1916) that I will discuss in detail in Chapters 6 and 8.

4

Destructive Narcissism: Fusion versus Idealization

DESTRUCTIVE NARCISSISM

Rosenfeld (1971) suggests that it is essential to differentiate between libidinal and destructive kinds of narcissism. He also emphasizes the need to put forward a theory of destructive narcissism, "completely neglected"—as he states—in both psychoanalytic theory and practice, perhaps because of a tendency to idealize destructive parts of the self, which become attractive because they stimulate feelings of omnipotence. He declares: "When destructive narcissism of this kind is a feature of a patient's character structure, libidinal (that is to say loving, caring, interdependent) object relationships and any wish on the part of the self to experience the need for an object and to depend on it are devalued, attacked, and destroyed *with pleasure*" (p. 22). There exists at the same time a process of idealization directed toward bad and destructive self objects, organized as a Mafia-like gang controlled by a leader that continuously exercises a "tyranny" over the rest of the objects with the use of different manipulations.

The tyranny of the bad idealized object is established in a complex manner, according to a narcissistic organization that attempts to maintain, with great violence, an omnipotent control of the good objects by means of successive degradation and profanation of the breast's goodness, vindictive hope, chameleonic or "as if" defenses, projection of the superego's primitive aspects, intrusive and paralyzing projective identifications, merciless attack on thinking, self-envy mechanisms, and so forth. However, before continuing, it makes sense to attempt a definition of the concept of narcissism, and leave for the next chapter the narcissistic organization and interaction of the internal objects.

It is, on the other hand, impossible to undertake the evaluation of narcissism without stumbling into the multiplicity of confusions and discrepancies the term implies. First, there is a *theoretical* contradiction determined by the old confusion between heredity (instinctive theory) and social acquisitions (object relations theory). Second, there is also a *clinical* confusion brought about by the mixture of descriptive and phenomenological issues with psychoanalytical and metapsychological ones. Finally, and very important, there is also a confusion about two different qualities of narcissism, capacity for *fusion* (drive, self, object, outside–inside reality, time, etc.) and a tendency to *idealize* (self and object). We should attempt a succinct investigation of all of them.

Theoretical Confusion

From an epigenetic perspective, a fracture between instinct and object is absolutely artificial. In a continuous

92

interaction the instinct, the ego, and the external world evolve together without contradictions, trapped by the forces of chance and determinism. "The fallacy," to quote Laplanche and Pontalis (1973), "made all the more flagrant by being expressed in 'biological' language . . . involves the following question: Just how are we supposed to picture the transition from a monad shut in upon itself to a progressive discovery of the object?" (p. 257). The issue is to conceive the object as the corollary of the instinctual drive within the context of the unconscious phantasy, a concept that implies that it will be absolutely impossible to conceive one without the other because they are two different faces of the same phenomenon. An objective answer to such an argument is the notion of epigenesis, as it is viewed within the realm of biology at large, and as a way out from the old dilemma of the chicken and the egg.

The question of where the object is at the early stage of development is very similar to the question posed by Piaget (1971) when he wonders where to locate the color of the eyes of a human embryo a few weeks after conception. Or, in a similar vein, I have often wondered if the final outcome of a dream is already implicit within the first images that appear at the beginning of the dream, or whether, in their progressive travel, the images will jump from perception to perception guided solely by chance. From a biological perspective, Piaget (1971) states:

> [If] it is difficult from the phylogenetic point of view, to conceive of man as preformed in bacterium or virus, it is every bit as hard to make out how, from the ontogenetic point of view, the main stages of "determination" or induction, and most important of the final functional "reintegration" of differentiated organs,

could already be present in the initial stages of segmentation. [p. 14]

Waddington (1957) compares epigenetic construction with the progression of a geometric theorem, where each step is rendered indispensable by the sum of those preceding it, though none is directly derived from the axioms underlying the original ones. Another form of comprehending these statements is to compare the concept of epigenesis with the creation of a river, and to wonder where the path is that the water must follow on its way to the sea before it starts to spring from the mountain? It seems as if the water and its path evolve together as the water tumbles down, rapidly and continuously probing the terrain's topography.

Epigenesis explains how a biological phenomenon is built on the basis of a paradox, which conjugates together and at the same time, like the two faces of Janus, the forces of *chance* on the one hand and of *determinism* on the other. Determinism allows the combining of only a limited number of elements or images. Chance, however, decides the direction of these combinations. How many dreams can be made, how many speeches expressed, or concerts composed with the same limited number of images, words, or sounds? In their beginning, elements combine by chance, but once an organization is achieved, it will be repeated by compulsion, a formula familiar to psychoanalysis in Freud's concept of repetition compulsion. The instinct, the ego, the superego, and the environment evolve together, influencing each other and slowly complicating their structures as the intricacy of the psychic apparatus reaches maturity. The ego present from the very beginning secures early and primitive object relations, even in utero (Aray 1985), different perhaps from the object relations observed at later ages, but object relations, nevertheless. Similarly, the superego also emerges earlier than Freud conceived it, perhaps different from the more consolidated superego of latency. Such a primitive superego will give room to the conception of a pregenital Oedipus, integrated of part objects and forerunner of a later Freudian Oedipus, organized on the basis of total and sexually differentiated persons.

According to the concept of epigenesis, it is impossible to conceive the breast apart from the act of feeding, because feeding is the only feasible way the instinct obtains satisfaction. From the point of view of object relations theory, the notions of "primary" and "secondary" narcissism are inconceivable, because the instinct cannot detach from the outside object, like a pseudopodium, and invest in the ego alone, as Freud (1914) once stated.

It is interesting, however, that Klein seldom referred to narcissism but for two short accounts in her papers "The Origins of Transference" (1952) and "Notes on Some Schizoid Mechanisms" (1946), where her statements appear more conciliatory than controversial, as she attempts to comply with classical psychoanalysis and to prove that Freud might have denied the existence of an objectless stage. Examining this situation from a historical perspective, one could speculate that Klein feared Freudian heresy at a time when her novel contributions to psychoanalysis were being so severely criticized.

Clinical Confusion

In 1914 Freud conceived narcissism as the *libidinal investment of the external object as well as the ego,* in a sort of pendular motion where the libido swayed either to the outside or to the inner world. Under the influence of the instinctive theory, the notion of narcissism was understood by Freud as a hereditary concept: born empty of the object (autoerotism and primary narcissism), the instinct is capable of unraveling on its own, as in a vacuum, to later cathect the outside object but also to break away from it during specific circumstances—such as psychosis—in order to invest in the ego (secondary narcissism). The concept of secondary narcissism appeared in Freud as an attempt to explain the clinical autistic withdrawal of psychotic patients, a notion now abandoned since researchers in the field of psychosis agree that such patients are capable also of a "transference psychosis" (Rosenfeld 1952).

In 1911 and later in 1914 and 1917, Freud defined primary narcissism as an intermediary and necessary libidinal step from autoerotism to erotism. Referring to "Senatspräsident" Schreber in 1911, he stated:

> What happens is this. There comes a time in the development of the individual at which he unifies his sexual instincts (which have hitherto been engaged in auto-erotic activities) in order to obtain a love-object; and he begins by taking himself, his own body, as his love-object, and only subsequently proceeds from this to the choice of some person other than himself as his object. [pp. 60–61]

Secondary narcissism, on the other hand, was described as the investment of the ego with object libido. Hartmann (1964), as well as Jacobson (1964), to mention only two, widened the ego's theoretical vision by introducing structural as well as representational concepts of the self, allowing Hartmann then to redefine narcissism, as the *libidinal investment of the self.* Secondary narcissism also induced the conception of another construct: the ego ideal, heir to childhood narcissism, according to Freud.

For Kohut (1971) and Kernberg (1989), it is not so much the direction of the libido—either to the external object or to the self—that determines the concept of narcissism, but the idealizing and inflating nature of the libido, linked to the concept of ego ideal, a condition Kohut has referred to as the "grandiose self." Kernberg (1975), on the other hand, claimed that such a conception leaves out the "aggressive impulses," compelling him to correct again the definition of narcissism as the *relative predominance of libido investment over aggressive investment*; and redefining as well the concept of libido (1989) "as the hierarchically supraordinate integration of positive affective investments of self and objects" (pp. 723–724).

It is obvious that all of these definitions, from Freud to Kernberg, including Hartmann, Jacobson, and Kohut, assimilate the concept of narcissism with the manic and omnipotent characteristics of the ego ideal, a condition only descriptive but not at all metapsychological, since such attributes denounce the symptomatological facade seen in those patients classified as "narcissistic personalities." In Kleinian terms, the expansive phenomenology observed in such patients' behavior represents the consequence of the internalized ideal object. Kernberg (1989), for instance, says that

> sometime between the ages of 3 and 5 years the
> narcissistic personality, instead of integrating positive

and negative representations of self and of objects, "on
the road to object constancy," puts together all the
positive representations and idealized representations
of self and objects, which results in an extremely
unrealistic and idealized concept of himself and a
pathologic, grandiose self. [p. 724]

We could ask, following a similar orientation, if the
incorporation of the bad object, as seen in melancholic
states, is not equally narcissistic, since this clinical entity
is also the consequence of a fusion between self and object,
similar to the condition we observe in "narcissistic personality."

Fusion and Idealization

More recently, Hanna Segal (1983) summarized Klein's
contributions on narcissism in the following manner:

> She (Klein) differentiates between narcissistic states
> and the narcissistic object relations and structure. The
> narcissistic states she relates to the withdrawal to an
> idealized internal object . . . The narcissistic object
> relations and structure she relates to projective iden-
> tification. Her view of narcissistic object relations con-
> tinues Freud's work on narcissistic object choice, but
> emphasizes also elements of control of an object im-
> plicit in the concept of projective identification. [p.
> 269]

But even in the slight accounts written by Klein about
narcissism, we could infer that her intention was directed
toward a conception different from that of classical theory.
In 1946 she stated:

> Another typical feature of schizoid object relations is their narcissistic nature which derives from the infantile introjective and projective processes. For, as I suggested earlier, when the ego-ideal is projected into another person, this person becomes predominantly loved and admired because he contains the good parts of the self. *Similarly, the relation to another person on the basis of projecting bad parts of the self into him is of a narcissistic nature, because in this case as well the object strongly represents one part of the self.* [p. 13; italics mine]

In this line of thinking, introjection of the idealized object (libidinal investment of the self) as we observe it in the narcissistic personality (Kernberg 1975, 1989), as well as introjection of the bad object (aggressive investment of the self) as seen in the melancholic states, are both consequences of a narcissistic fusion between self-representations and the internalized external object, organized as a structure I will soon discuss as the "narcissistic conglomerate."

It is unfortunate that Freud described narcissism only in terms of his concept of libido and that he never revised the notion after 1920 when he began to emphasize the significance of the death instinct. This narrowly focused formulation of narcissism (based on the idealizing quality of the incorporation of the object libido—in Freudian and ego psychology terminology—or ideal object, in Kleinian terms) is responsible for persisting confusion over the artificial distinction between drive and object. This confusion licensed the adulteration of psychoanalytical metapsychology with psychiatric phenomenology, institutionalizing a clinical entity now widely known as narcissistic personality, which is based on the inflated introjection of the ideal object. According to Fairbairn (1952), the introjection of the idealized object (as seen in manic states) requires the compulsion to project the bad object, which when introjected—and this occurs very often (bipolar pathology)—changes into a depressive condition that in Kleinian metapsychology is also narcissistic.

We need to be able to discern and clarify what exactly defines narcissism: either the inflated introjection of the ideal object (object libido), or the fusion of different part self-objects, or both.

PERVERSE AND DESTRUCTIVE NARCISSISM

I will refer to pathological narcissism only as the pathological form of the paranoid-schizoid position, where the intensity of the death instinct shatters the object into extreme parts of very good or idealized objects, and very bad or persecutory ones. Originally, the good object is idealized by the ego as a defense in order to compensate for the pain produced by the frustration of the bad object (Klein 1946). This explains why the idealized object so closely mirrors the bad one, just like Narcissus and his own image on the surface of the water. Even though both part objects are closely interrelated, they must also remain separated and distinct from each other to avoid the good object possibly being destroyed by the envy of the bad. Such a separation is guaranteed by omnipotent processes of projection, introjection, and identification. If a part object, bad or idealized, is introjected within the self, its congruent (mirror-image) counterpart must be projected into the outside object. In order to guarantee that such splitting will be preserved, the projection must be supported by a mechanism of identification, meaning that both part objects, good and bad, should be anchored, not only within the self (introjective identification) but also in the outside object (projective identification).

In the original myth, Narcissus is punished by Nemesis, falls in love with his own reflection, and remains helpless beside the water, trying to touch his image. He is unable to move himself away from it until it is transformed into a river flower. The prophecy of Tiresias the seer is fulfilled: "that Narcissus will live a long life only if he never knows himself," just like the myth of Dracula—unable to see himself in the mirror.

The metapsychology of narcissistic object relations consists of a complex organization I call the "narcissistic conglomerate," which involves the double fusion of part-self and part-object representations, placed internally (the "internal cluster" product of introjective identifications), and a congruent or mirror cluster, also formed by fused part-self and part-object representations, placed outside in the external object (the "external cluster" product of projective identification). In other words, a particular narcissistic conglomerate is formed of an internal cluster plus a congruent mirror structure, the external cluster. The clusters are integrated by fusion of part-self and part-object representations. The position of both clusters, internal and external, may exchange within the schizo-paranoid position, but distance between them is always preserved. The need to preserve this distance will determine the clinical rigidity and pathological character of that particular structure. A patient, for instance, might be struggling with the pain induced by the existence of an internal narcissistic cluster formed by an excluded-abandoned-envious-child, while at the same time projecting in the analyst a congruent and external cluster made of a loved-abundant-independent-object, experienced in the transference. Induced by the suffering, the patient might take holidays a few days before the analyst in order to invert the narcissistic organization.

We learn from Bion that this kind of object interaction within the pathological narcissistic organization is extremely complex, more so even than I have described thus far, because those narcissistic clusters constitute, according to him, high-speed particles or "beta elements," good only to be expelled or acted out instead of being used as material for thinking. The interaction between these part objects has also been described by Steiner (1981) as perverted in nature. The main purpose of this pathological organization is to establish control of the internal world, a tyranny of the mental apparatus, preserving the organization and continuously destroying any opposition, either by seduction, threat, coercion, deceit, or most of all, "revengeful hope," Monte Cristo style.[1] Preservation of life, peaceful harmony, long-term tranquility, and so forth are continuously denigrated and devalued to the point that not only is logical symbolism obstructed but cause–effect relationships are inverted. *Action is measured more by its intention than by its consequences:* after-effects of drugs are marvelous, all-night parties, are fantastic, injected

---

[1]A detailed discussion of this concept is given in the next chapter.

drugs superb. Secondary consequences are completely denied: loss of work or studies, robbery, troubles with the police, family conflicts, crime, prostitution—the list goes on. "Badness" is idealized and negative identification, such as delinquency, drug addiction, or any kind of destructive acting out, is sold to the ego as an expression of the true self.

A patient involved in a long history of delinquent actions and drug consumption had managed to change to the point of creating his own business and giving up drugs completely for three years following a long commitment to a therapeutic community. He had been in analysis for two years and was doing reasonably well, aside from some occasional acting out. We had managed to understand some of the processes of internal splitting—the existence of a part object we referred to as the "drugged one," representing the structure of the narcissistic "gang" or pathological narcissism; the inner struggle to deny any feeling of dependency; the exaltation of omnipotent behavior; and so forth. We also explored the hypothesis that the drugged one was a revengeful part of him that tried to destroy the "good son" he felt his parents wanted him to be. Two weeks before the summer holidays he brought the following dream: *He was walking with his girlfriend on a dark street and was afraid of being mugged, when suddenly three individuals jumped out of a corner, put a gun to his head, and said: "Don't you move, this is an assault." He was scared they would take a chain and medal he wore around his neck, which was very important*

103

to him because it was given to him by his mother when he was a child. The thought in the dream of the chain been taken away made him very depressed. His associations brought memories from the time he was an assailant and had once tried to rob a drug dealer, was almost shot by him, and was later caught by the police. He recalled as well a time when three thugs tried to mug him; he got into a fistfight with them and managed to disarm them, but was chased afterward and feared being shot. The chain and medal he was wearing were associated with his good aspects: the good son his parents wanted him to be. I told him that he was very concerned about me going away because he feared being mugged inside, by the envious part object that we named the drugged one, and robbed of the chain, meaning his desire to be the "good patient" he felt I wanted him to be, or again, the good son, a possibility that made him very depressed.

Because the intimate structure of narcissistic organizations or the narcissistic conglomerate is so closed and complex, perhaps a detailed description of a session with a borderline patient will help to illustrate these theoretical contributions.

Leslie was a 32-two-year-old single female, in analysis for two years. Unable to form a lasting relationship with a man, she had managed to stay with one boyfriend, whom I will refer to as Bob, for eight months. However, she was very ambivalent about him and often compared him with Charles, a former boyfriend who abandoned her about five years before in order to marry another woman. Although she criticized Bob as being childish, unkempt, dirty, smelly, and unsophisticated, she remained with him because he was nice and tender with her. In contrast, she remembered Charles as professional, well educated, sophisticated, and a successful musician. She followed his career closely, and often experienced great pain, in spite of the time elapsed, whenever she saw his picture in the newspaper or on television. Not only did the image of this unreachable, magnificent person produce pain and envy in her, but her own feelings of rejection toward Bob were unbearable. She called me several times just to tell me that she was very negative about Bob, or she used the session with a cathartic purpose, discharging her negative feelings as a "toilet breast"—to use Meltzer's (1967) expression—expecting me to act as a catalytic agent, or some kind of alchemist, capable of changing her destructive and envious feelings into good ones. At other moments she resorted to more drastic defenses of extrojection and ran to the bathroom obviously distressed. On one occasion these mechanisms became more obvious after she presented a dream in which a cat was defecating outside of my office and a man was checking to make sure that the cat was covering the feces in order to conceal the smell. Idealization of the transference was a necessary measure in order to guarantee that I was not going to fail in my role of continuously concealing her feces, meaning, to free her from any envious or destructive feelings she might be experiencing. As the analysis unfolded, doubts started to appear, as she feared my becoming uninterested or bored, and falling asleep. At the end of a session, she turned back and saw me with my eyes closed, confirming her suspicions of my lack of interest. In the next session, she brought the following dream: *She was walking inside of a room. There was a lady sitting with a cat on her lap. The cat appeared very angry and threatening, showing its fangs. She came into the room feeling very frightened. The lady then got water from a pail next to her and wet the cat's mouth, relaxing its muscles and changing the expression to a pleasant one. She then felt more relaxed as she approached the lady.*

In her associations, she identified me as the lady with the cat and herself with her own frightened image in the dream. Relaxing the cat's muscles with the water obviously constituted her attempt at repressing her aggressive impulses because of her fear of verbalizing them.

In the narcissistic structure, an aggressive part of the self, fused with the part object frightening-lady-with-the-cat, (projected narcissistic cluster) is projected, and also fused with the outside object—the analyst—while at the same time a mirror reflection of the object, a "frightened" part of the self, remains inside, fused with the self (introjected narcissistic cluster). There is a developmental common ground between both idealized and bad objects, because idealization is always used by the ego as a compensation in order to fend off the frustrating aspects of the bad object. Both part objects, idealized and bad, share common developmental roots. Within the schizo-paranoid position both part objects remain separated by means of

projective and introjective mechanisms (due also to instinctive defusion, Rosenfeld 1971), while at the same time
they also preserve the mirror quality of their primitive and
original organization. Mobility of cathexis is another important quality of projective and introjective identification
in this kind of pathological narcissism: at a given moment
it could switch places easily, and what was outside becomes inside and vice versa. If the "relaxing" capacity of
the water in Leslie's dream was to fail, the analyst would
become the frightened part and Leslie the frightening one.

In the original myth, as predicted by Tiresias, Narcissus disappeared when confronted with his own reflection on the surface of the water. A metaphor that perhaps
underlines that narcissism fades away as the ego com-
pletes itself by rescuing those parts of the self placed in the
outside object by means of projective identification. The
reduction of annihilatory anxieties by the power of insight
allows the ego to reduce the debilitating defense of projective identification by bringing within its boundaries those
parts that have been projected. As the need for extreme
idealization diminishes, and the good and the bad part
objects are placed in the same space inside the internal
world, a transitional situation is created that permits,
following Klein, the establishment of the depressive position. Whenever narcissistic object relations are undone,
differentiation between inner and outer worlds becomes
better delineated. The other and the self fill themselves
progressively, slowly emerging as separate entities.

Rescuing the projected parts of the self is often not a
silent event, perceived by the patient as feelings of strange-
ness, anxiety, or controlled micropsychotic reactions
during the analytical session. The ego, however, not only

has to meet and resolve the threats of an annihilatory separation anxiety as it advances to maturity, but also the anxiety of exclusion that takes place once the ego becomes aware of the existence of a different object outside.[2] Such exclusion anxiety underscores the presence of the Oedipus complex's triangular interaction.

Oedipal object relations evolve hand in hand with narcissistic object relations. Three different phenomena may be considered possible forerunners of the triangular and three-dimensional interaction of the Oedipus complex: the instinctive defusion between libidinal and aggressive drives present in primitive forms of object relations; following such a defusion, the splitting of the ego and of the object between bad and idealized parts. The instinctive defusion allows the ideal object to be invested with libido and the bad one with death wishes (Rosenfeld 1971); finally, the ego's cognitive capacity between the ages of 6 to 8 months to mentally represent the outside object in absentia and to recognize it as a separate entity from the self.

The internal representation of the object as a separate entity evolves next to the narcissistic object relations already present, manufacturing a condition where a separate object exists next to a part object narcissistically fused with a part of the self, in the manner already described. Klein has conceptualized the notion of narcissistic object

---

[2]Obviously, the main purpose of interpretation in general is to make conscious the unconscious, to return what has been projected, and so forth; and there are different forms of how this is to be achieved. One of the these techniques is discussed in Chapter 8 as the interpretation of self-envy.

relations within the structure of the Oedipus complex as the presence of the "combined parental figure," a phantasy the child projects onto the parents as he visualizes them in a "continuous intercourse," where oral, anal, and genital gratifications are exchanged (Klein 1932, Segal 1964).

5

Orestes versus Oedipus

Who feareth envy, feareth to be great.

Aeschylus: *Clytemnestra*

LIBIDO CONTRA AGGRESSION

As we have seen, aggression has not met, in classical psychoanalysis, with the same ubiquitous agreement as did libido. And current debate in the psychoanalytical congresses over ego psychology as practiced in North America and object relations theory, more common in Europe and South America, is far from being settled. Many of the arguments sustained in the past about this controversy still hold true. The problem is not determined by a territorial disparity, a cultural discrepancy, or a traditional compromise, like belonging to different political parties or rooting for rival football teams: in spite of human limita-

113

tions regarding such abstract matters, [the mind should be grasped as a whole.] It is furthermore impossible to conceive the idea of a self-envy mechanism if we do not also contemplate the existence of a death instinct or of a drive toward self destruction. Let us assume that there was a historical mistake, in the sense that Freud did not officially recognize until 1920 the importance played by the death instinct in the dualistic interaction of the unconscious. Following this same line, Peter Gay (1988) said about Freud:

> What came to puzzle him, then, as it puzzled others, was only why he should hesitate to elevate aggressiveness into a rival of libido. "Why have we ourselves," he asked later, looking back, "needed such a long time before we decide to recognize an aggressive drive?" A little ruefully he recalled his own defensive rejection of such a drive when the idea first appeared in the psychoanalytic literature, and "how long it took before I became receptive to it" . . . In those years [concluded Gay] Freud had simply not been ready. [p. 396]

The first attempt to describe the death instinct on equal footing with the sexual was perhaps produced by Sabina Spielrein, a Russian doctor who, after a psychotic break, was "successfully" analyzed by Jung at Burgholzli from 1904 to 1908, becoming afterward his mistress. In 1911 she presented a paper to Freud and his group at the Wednesday meeting in Vienna, with the suggestive title of "Die Destruktion als Ursache des Werdens" (Destruction as the Cause of Becoming), about which, in a letter to Jung dated March 21, 1912, Freud had this to say:

> As for Spielrein's paper, I know only the one chapter that she read at the Society. She is very bright; there is

meaning in everything she says; her destructive drive is not much to my liking, because I believe it is personally conditioned. She seems abnormally ambivalent. [Van Waning, 1992, p. 405]

In August of 1911, three months before Spielrein presented her paper, Freud had his final clash with Adler over Freud's contention that Adler was attempting to introduce a new kind of psychoanalysis by magnifying aggression and deemphasizing libido and infantile sexuality.

Once angry, Freud stayed angry [about this affair]. He had long patiently listened to Adler, but no more. In this mood, he could not recognize that some of Adler's ideas, like his postulate of an independent aggressive drive, might be valuable contributions to psychoanalytic thought. Rather, he bestowed on Adler the most damaging psychological terms in his vocabulary. [Gay 1988, pp. 222–223]

Was Spielrein's contribution then completely ignored at that time as an immediate consequence of the Freud-Adler affair, or because she was a woman, or a foreigner, because she had a psychotic breakdown, or because she was Jung's mistress, or perhaps everything together? Immediately after praising her paper in a letter addressed to her, Jung hypocritically also wrote to Freud quoting Horace, the Latin poet, in these terms: "I was working on Spielrein's paper just before my departure. One must say: *desinat in piscem mulier formosa superne.*[1] In 1920,

---

[1]"What at the top is a lovely woman ends below in a fish" (McGuire 1974, p. 498).

when Freud finally changed from a monistic emphasis on
the libido to a dualistic conception of sexual as well as
aggressive drives, he accorded some small recognition to
Spielrein, when in a footnote in Chapter 6 of *Beyond the
Pleasure Principle*, he stated:

> A considerable portion of these speculations have been
> anticipated by Sabina Spielrein (1912) in an instruc-
> tive and interesting paper which, however, is unfortu-
> nately not entirely clear to me. She there describes the
> sadistic components of the sexual instinct as "destruc-
> tive." [p. 55]

Ten years later, in *Civilization and Its Discontents*,
Freud (1930) had this to say: "I remember my own defensive attitude when the idea of an instinct of destruction
first emerged in psychoanalytic literature, and how long it
took before I became receptive to it" (p. 120). Freud may
have been referring to Spielrein's paper again, since the
presentation of a 27-year-old even eight years before would
have registered in his memory. Others believe, however,
although Freud himself denied it, that it took a worldwide
conflagration such as World War I for Freud to became
aware of the inconceivable amount of aggression harbored
within the human spirit. Perhaps it was difficult to imagine
such wrath during the epoch of a peaceful Europe and a
gentle Vienna, where the main clinical issues brought to
the consulting room were the fear of pregnancy in an
already large family, onanism, masturbation, repressed
sexuality, hysterical symptomatology, and psychosis. Although Freud remained faithful to the dualistic instinctive

theory to the very end of his life, his delay in recognizing it produced perhaps the most important controversy within the development of psychoanalysis. In this same vein, Laplanche and Pontalis (1973) declared: "The notion of death instinct . . . has not managed to gain the acceptance of his disciples and successors in the way that the majority of his conceptual contributions have done—and it is still one of the most controversial of psychoanalytic concepts" p. 97.

At the thirty-sixth International Psychoanalytical Congress in Rome, Dr. Robert Wallerstein invited all psychoanalysts to submit reports describing a period of work with a patient and the relevant background, as well as details about what each actually said to the other and the analyst's reactions to the interchange. The *International Journal of Psycho-Analysis* (volume 72, 1991), published several papers that followed Wallerstein's suggestion. The first of these articles was by Dr. Scott Carder from California, and just as the editors of the journal did, I have chosen it as a paradigm of the North American psychoanalytical approach, conscious all the while of the dangers of reductionism.

The case presented was of a 40-year-old housewife with a quick temper who developed a symptomatology of fatigue and numbness, as well as a heavy drinking habit, after her significantly older husband suffered a near-fatal heart attack while traveling overseas. Just before the beginning of her analysis, the patient and another girlfriend spent a lot of time together talking about their desire to have an affair with Dan, a handsome mutual friend. The patient was the second of four siblings, with an older sister and two younger brothers. At the age of 16, she fell in love with a friend of her father who was much older than she was.

From this background we might construct two possible transferential hypotheses:

(1) A monistic approach that considers only the presence of a nonambivalent, pure libidinal interaction: An oedipal infatuation is presumed from both her boyfriend's age when she was 16 and her present husband, as well as from her relationship with her parents. Her symptomatology (fatigue, numbness, and drinking) could be related to her fear of losing her beloved husband-father. Her desire to have an affair with another man could be interpreted as a need to preserve the derivatives of the oedipal relationship by finding a replacement owing to her husband's life-threatening ailment. The split-off material will be related to repressed libidinal aspects of the oedipal relationship. The analyst's aim might be oriented to deal with the anxiety produced by the threat of her husband's possible death, and to clarify the oedipal nature of the transference.

(2) A dualistic approach, which incorporates the existence of both sexual and death drives: The transference in this case is conceived quite differently. The presenting symptomatology is the result of feelings of guilt and persecution because the patient's death wish toward her husband father is very nearly realized (observed also in her desire to have an affair, or in the affair she *already* has in her own fantasies). She fears that she could be discovered and punished, so she is punishing herself instead. She has ambivalent feelings toward her father, whom she needs and loves but at the same time wishes to possess, control, attack, and destroy out of envy, because he preferred her

118

mother. The material repressed will be related to the split-off feelings of aggression, observed in her need to seduce the analyst-father in order to control him as well, and to destroy the analytical marriage.

In the session presented the patient starts by saying: "Yesterday when I came in I said, 'You look great.' I was surprised it was so casual and spontaneous. I like it, but it scares me. It was the way I would talk to a friend." At this moment the analyst intervenes and asks: "What are you afraid of?" He explains that by doing so, he is inviting her to investigate the apprehension that these feelings are creating in her. It is quite possible that the analyst was achieving this, but it may be as well that the patient was experiencing it as an invitation to continue her seduction, meaning that the analyst was responding to a projective identification that has unconsciously induced him to ask questions. The patient insists that her fear might be the consequence of liking him too much, but complains that she does not really know him very well, and the analyst inquires if she experiences with him the "same holding back" that she says she feels with her friend Dan. She accepts the interpretation, but states that her husband would be "devastated" if he were to find out about her inner feelings, immediately expressing that if her husband were to die, she would demand much more from Dan than she had obtained from her husband. Then she said: "What a basket case I would be if John [her husband] were to die during my analysis." In a remark made outside the session, Dr. Calder explained that Mrs. C. is sharing her concern about her husband's possible death because he provides sex and love as well as a "father–daughter relationship." Later in the same session Mrs. C. comments about the similarity of the ambivalence she feels about Dan and her husband: "I both wanted and did not want it. My husband said his heart attack in South America was due to the stress of being away from home, but he was really worried about Dan and me and he repressed it." Following this statement she expresses her concern that the analysis was not going to go on forever. "Besides, (she continues) you wouldn't want it to go on forever and I will have to deal with ending it." She complains angrily that she should have never started analysis, but accepts that it is already too late for such a protest. At the end of the session the analyst states that perhaps she is feeling like a victim in analysis because she does not have any other choice.

It seems, as Betty Joseph (1989) has remarked, that there are two different analyses here, one the patient is attempting to do, perhaps as a form of complying, and a secret one not yet uncovered:

> Sometimes we can see the listening or observing part of the patient emerging clearly as a perverse part, which uses interpretative work for purposes of perverse excitement. These patients provocatively "misunderstand" interpretations, take words out of context, and attempt to disturb or arouse the analyst. [p. 80]

What I think is missing in the analysis of Mrs. C., is the uncovering of that perverted part that attempts a complicity with the analyst, in order *not to know* about her true desire to kill [her father-husband-analyst], as a revenge for oedipal exclusion, as well as the persecutory anxiety induced by such fantasies and the appearance of symptoms as perhaps a form of neutralizing the superego castrating threats projected outside. In other words, the uncovering of the repressed death wishes and split-off components are not dealt with at all, as if they do not represent for the analyst the same interest that the libidinal aspects do. This is made very clear in the final remarks of the paper's discussion, when Dr. Calder interpreted that her symptoms of "numbness and weakness" in her lower extremities appeared once she became apprehensive about her husband's possible death, and that they were also related to the transference as the possibility of losing her analyst. The symptoms were also conceived as an inability to "stand on her own and assume independent and adult responsibility."

What exactly is responsible for such scotomization of clinical as well as theoretical conceptualizations of the death instinct, within the psychoanalytical praxis, in some important schools of psychoanalysis? Is it perhaps Freud's long-term delay in placing both drives on equal terms, the forces of Thanatos and the forces of Eros? Or the unhappy option of referring to this conceptualization in *Beyond the Pleasure Principle* as a "biological speculation" (Segal 1993)? In this quest, however, we will not leave out the importance of well-known contributions from psychoanalysts such as Fenichel, Hartmann, Kris, and Loewenstein, who seriously opposed Freud's giving the death and sexual instincts equal weight, and who also had a strong influence on the North American psychoanalytical movement. There is as well the long and passionate debate between Klein and Anna Freud, which in the end strongly induced and influenced the need to choose between one party or the other, between those dissident followers of Klein and those faithful to Freud and his daughter. It is quite possible that this contention might also have created a discrepancy over issues related to the death drive, since Klein was alone in taking Freud's death instinct and all its implications to heart.

> Until very recently, the majority of North American psychoanalysts completed their training without having even heard of Melanie Klein's name. After all, Anna Freud was the daughter of the Master, and many North Americans had the tendency to treat her as if she had inherited some of his genius. [Grosskurth 1986, p. 405]

ORESTES VERSUS OEDIPUS

There is no question that Freud was inspired by genius when he chose the Oedipus complex as the central myth of any emotional conflict, neurotic as well as psychotic. However, the Oedipus myth appears to be guided more by fate than by revenge, weighing more the incestuous aspect of the complex than the aggressive one, reflected in the parricide committed by Oedipus at the beginning of his dis-adventure. Or in Green's words (1975): "like the return of the repressed, he [Oedipus] is irresistibly inclined to come back to its center: to Jocasta's bed" (pp. 355–364).

Orestes, on the other hand, is not a myth of fate but one of pure mayhem and vengeance, closer in that sense to human emotions and tragedy. This may be why Klein (1963) chose to scrutinize this myth in her posthumously published paper on the *Oresteia*, in which the metapsychology of primitive envy is depicted as enclosed within the oedipal domain, but is not, as others have assumed, the representation of a negative Oedipus. The main aspect of the myth of Orestes is Orestes' feeling of revenge against his mother, fostered by both himself and his sister Electra, for selecting his cousin Aegisthus instead of himself. From this perspective Orestes is not responding to a negative Oedipus complex organization, that is, to a passive surrender to his father as well as anger against his mother for destroying the target of his desire. Instead, the murder of Clytemnestra is an expression of pure envy—Orestes cannot forgive her betrayal. After all, she has not killed his father in order to fulfil Orestes' Oedipus complex but to favor someone other than her son. It is not the bed of Agamemnon that Orestes seeks, but his mother's, just as Oedipus did; and his rage against both Clytemnestra and Aegisthus, her lover, is only an expression of jealousy and envious revenge, which "sparks the heart with a lust for the blood of the other in order to collapse both into nothing," (p. 19) as Emery (1992) puts it. This envy, then, is the expression of Orestes experiencing himself completely excluded from the possibility of fulfilling his desire of remaining his mother's narcissistic complement, something that will make him immune to any castration anxiety. I will discuss this aspect in the next chapter, where I refer to the "basic delusion," or the belief that the mother's lack of a penis is complemented by the child; however, since this delusion is always doomed to frustration, constrained by the limitations of reality, there is the phantasy that someone else might complement the mother's lack. Orestes' narcissistic rage is just the expression of the same failure, the difficulty in recognizing that the basic delusion cannot be fulfilled. This is why Orestes cannot forgive his mother's duplicity. From this point of view, Electra's and Orestes' motivation for killing their mother might come from different sides of their Oedipus complex: in Electra, loss of the possibility of fulfilling her incestuous desire toward her father, and Orestes, revenge over being excluded. Here I depart from Klein's (1963) and Green's (1975) evaluations of the myth of Orestes.

6

Revengeful versus Depressive Hope

Jan was a boy who once found, by chance, that "the mighty ocean was leaking through a small hole in the city's dike. Even a naughty boy like Jan knew that a small leak unchecked would get bigger and that if the dike should give way a terrible flood might drown the whole town. . . . He then wrapped the handkerchief around his finger and dug it into the tiny gap in the earthen wall. The sun was going down, but for now, at least the flow stopped." When the people discovered what he had done, "the town held a great festival to honor the young hero who had saved everybody from the worst flood since Noah."

"The Boy Who Held Back the Sea" (a Dutch story)

BASIC DELUSION, INDISPENSABILITY (EXCEPTION), AND REVENGEFUL HOPE

What guides and sustains the destructive purpose of pathological narcissism in order to maintain its tyranny and control over most of the functioning ego, as seen in narcissistic or borderline patients? What fosters the process of idealization of the bad object, while at the same time undermining the importance of the good one? The narcissistic structure of some patients considered as borderline or narcissistic seems to be organized around a powerful force, guided according to a hope based on revenge, or "revengeful hope"—of which the Count of Monte Cristo is a paradigm—directed against envied self-objects projected in the transference. A significant aspect of the ego feels enslaved to this organization—the "narcissistic gang," to use Rosenfeld's expression—and important decisions in a person's life are made in response to it. This vengeance appears to be the consequence of a disavowal of the terrible pain and anxiety induced by oedipal exclusion and fear of castration, and may be based on the omnipotent delusion or belief, that it might be possible to achieve the narcissistic and infantile desire to fulfill the mother's "basic narcissistic injury," or lack of a penis—that the baby will be *indispensable* to completing the mother's narcissistic "fault." I call this condition the "basic delusion." Feelings of indispensability are normal, and even necessary, to sustain the natural symbiosis between mother and child. But when such feelings are increased due to the mother's need to fulfill her own castration anxiety as well as her phallic envy, followed, at the same time, by an early birth of another sibling, the need for indispensability reaches the level of a powerful omnipotence used to restore the basic delusion and, further on, to reach the level of a pathological and destructive narcissistic organization. This whole organization will then be guided by a powerful feeling of revenge, a revenge sold to the ego as the only hope, as an all-or-nothing kind of solution for continuous suffering.

This revengeful hope is also sustained by a paradox that threatens, like a trap or a Catch-22 dilemma, the possibility of fulfilling the basic delusion: if the mother needs the child to remedy her biological fault, it will mean that she does not have a penis, that she is in reality castrated, which then implies that disavowal fails and castration is possible. But if, on the other hand, she does not require the child because she "has" her own penis (phantasy of the phallic mother), then the child is not indispensable and castration is also possible. The threat introduced by such a dilemma induces the need for further defense mechanisms such as splitting and idealization (ego ideal), in the shape of suspiciousness: someone else might be able to carry out the basic delusion and complement the mother's biological fault. Such a presumption causes a high level of anxiety as well as intense feelings of envy. Revengeful hope is then based on the possibility of destroying such a rival or threat: if that were to be obtained (meaning the destruction of the rival), the basic delusion might be possible. If the idealized object (the one capable of fulfilling the basic delusion) is projected—via projective identification—envy will be directed toward the outside object; but if it is introjected—via introjective identification—destructiveness will then be turned against the constructive aspects of the self, giving place to the appearance of self-envy mechanisms, a concept I will discuss further later on.

In some borderline patients, the specific characteristics of their basic delusion are given by the special profile provided by their mother's unconscious phantasy in relation to her own castration anxiety and defenses, such as phallic envy. Very often, mothers of this type of patient use schizoid mechanisms to deal with such feelings of envy, for example, Deutsch's "as if" or Winnicott's false self. I have described them as the "salamander's tail" (López-Corvo 1992, 1993), alluding to that particular capacity of certain kinds of lizards that when threatened give up a part of their tail, which will twist continuously in order to deceive the predator while the reptile hides in a safer place. Basically, these patients suffer from a disturbance in the *natural order of their desire*: they fancy the Other's desire, instead of their own, ready to please in a chameleonic fashion, incessantly changing and adapting to fulfill the Other's expected desire, but only as a defense to hide themselves, like the lizard, in order to avoid castration anxiety. Secretly, some of these patients conceal a revengeful and poisonous penis hidden in their anus among the feces, where nobody—they feel—will ever imagine locating it, representing in some addicted patients the phantasy of a "fecal phallus" (López-Corvo 1993). In the symbiotic interaction with their mother, these borderline patients attempt to fulfill their basic delusion by becoming themselves her fecal phallus; the drug in certain cases serves this purpose: to live inside the mother's anus, feeding on feces, as Meltzer (1966) has described.

In summary, the destructive and narcissistic organization of the self exercises its power over the ego by means of a hope based only on revenge; the feeling sold to the ego that negative identification (acting out, revenge, etc.) is exactly the true self; a hope directed at fulfilling the basic delusion as well as impeding others, out of envy, from fulfilling the delusion; a hope based on the all-or-nothing possibility, feeling like either God or a worm, and nothing in between; a compulsion for sameness and a terror of differences.

THE CASE OF HANNA

Hanna was 28 years old, single, three years older than her only brother, presenting a borderline structure whose dynamics within the analytical setting fit well the profile of a negative therapeutic reaction. In general, the revengeful hope was based on the continual need to control and castrate the object in order to possess its omnipotence and to fulfill a feeling of emptiness and melancholy.

In spite of the intense anxiety she continually displayed during sessions, she rejected my interpretations, holding obstinately to her own way of thinking, determining in this manner the dynamics of the narcissistic quality of object relations that took place in the transferential interaction. She regularly received my interpretations as severe criticism, real accusations, with no other purpose but to make her feel bad. She projected split-off bad part objects and bad parts of the self, while attempting to preserve within the self the idealized aspects. Whenever this defense failed, she reacted with anxiety and depression. Countertransferentially, I felt the impact of the projective identifications as feelings of anger. As often described in relation to negative therapeutic reactions, I felt frustrated and impotent, as the analytical instrument was paralyzed by her continual envious attacks. She unconsciously desired to seduce in order to control because of a wish to castrate the masculine omnipotent object (penis envy), to steal its power and to incorporate it in order to rid herself of empty castrated feelings. She consulted friends and other colleagues about what was going on in the analysis, and in one circumstance asked if she could invite one of them to witness the session. She complained that she had not made any progress and often voiced her desire to discontinue her analysis, a situation that contrasted with her regular attendance and intense interest about psychoanalytical issues. Other times, she presented the material incompletely, inducing countertransferentially the desire to inquire, to demand more information, giving the impression of keeping an important secret, perhaps related to the analysis or the analyst, re-creating an obscure and diffuse scenario, where I felt like a voyeur, curious and tempted. If I wanted more information, I might have to get closer, to question, often giving the impression of witnessing a primary scene. Early in the analysis, she shared some masturbatory fantasies, which portrayed a singular condensation: she imagined herself lying naked in an isolated alley raped and bleeding while it was raining. Although such a fantasy was felt as sexually arousing, at the same time it had the transferential purpose of eliciting feelings of pity and forgiveness, as anybody who would witness such a scene would never imagine that she was deriving a masochistic pleasure from it. There was a perverse purpose behind this phantasy: the seductive attempt in the transference or provoking incestuous desires, which could always be easily projected, because she could immediately state that she was a poor victim and that any sexual connotation came from the analyst and not from her. A similar phantasy was pictured of her being naked with a knife inside her vagina.

Very early in her analysis she had the following

dream: *Her boyfriend had both of his hands bandaged and she had to dress him like a baby, although he was a man also. She was feeding him with a spoon. Then they arrived at a restaurant and she feared to be seen with him. They sat in the corner, their backs to the other clients, and she started to feed him again.* After a short silence she stated that the interpretation I had given her the session before, where I said that sex was something to be hidden, did not apply to her problem.

There seemed to be a need to degrade a masculine part, to make it appear useless, like a baby—but who was, in any case, a man—and to project it in the transference, as we could infer from her comments about my interpretation from the previous session. If she was ashamed of her boyfriend's helplessness, she could have chosen any other place to feed him—after all it was her own dream—but she selected a public place like a restaurant, where she could "hide" in a corner, but from where she could also be seen. A similar situation was taking place in the transference, where the powerful feeding-mother was kept inside, and the masculine-helpless part, or baby aspect, was projected; at the same time, through her continual attacks on the interpretations, she was tying my hands too. In her phantasy she wanted others to observe how "helpless" I was; she wanted to invite somebody else to witness the analysis. It was an envious attack on both her own masculine self part, projected often, as well as *her younger rival brother.*

The struggle between the narcissistic gang, guided by feelings of revengeful hope on one hand, and the possibility of gratefulness or a depressive hope, on the other, was observed several months afterward, during the first

133

session following one week of holidays, when she stated that she wanted to say something nice to me, to welcome me, but then changed her feelings and said that she felt terrible and wanted to commit suicide. I felt that for the first time in the analysis she allowed herself to be nice and to welcome me with gratitude, to let me know how pleased she was to see me again, the *hope* of a warm relationship based on forgiveness. However, during the silence of her pause the anxiety appeared, the envious and destructive attack from an internal narcissistic gang that closes the "opening" and cancels the possibility of giving in to the compromise of a good working alliance, of a creative harmony and a depressive hope. Then I said to her that she seemed to be confused about what to give to me, to provide me with a nice welcome and to let me know how happy she felt to see me again, or to make me feel terrible, perhaps because of the anger she might have experienced due to my absence. "I feel terrible," she answered, "I am always doing it wrong, I am always destroying, I am good for nothing. I don't want to do that to you." She was crying bitterly. Countertransferentially, my feelings also changed. Instead of the anger I experienced previously, I felt the desire to apologize. But instead I decided to denounce the internal and envious gang. I said that she was struggling inside with a part that felt very envious of the loving feelings she could have for me, as if an angry part of her felt envious of a loving part also inside of her, as a conflict not so much with me, but between two different parts of her. She agreed and became obviously calmer.

Shortly after she remembered a dream in which I was very angry at her, took her by the neck, and while shaking her told her that I was fed up with her. The projection is also an important defense of the narcissistic gang, to place the enemy outside. I think that this dream was a response to my previous interpretation that the conflict was an internal one. At the next session she brought another dream: *I was walking inside of a tunnel with a girlfriend. I was just talking to her when I realized that you were also walking behind, and I feared that you might have listened to what I was telling her, something that I can no longer recollect.*

She provided no associations, and after a pause protested rather angrily that she wanted me to say something, anything, that she just wanted my approval. I felt that her wish for me to say something not only fostered the simple desire of making me present, but also of exercising an omnipotent control, that if I said something, she would have the opportunity of rejecting it. Perhaps this is what she fears for me to hear in her dream: she wants to keep me "behind her," in the tunnel, in her anus, to make me appear and disappear at her own will like her feces. But I also think that there is an opening, a little hope that the tight anal narcissistic structure could give in, that I could "hear," that is, that I could find out about the true nature of her omnipotent defenses, that what she wished to hide could be known: the revengeful hope based on childhood defenses against separation anxiety. Just like the reel game played by Freud's grandson, she will make me present to make me disappear. There seemed to be at the same time and at the same place, within the symbolism of her dream, the need to hide, to repress, on the one hand, and the possibility of listening, of knowing, on the other.

A few days later she arrived abruptly at the consulting room outside of her regular hour, obviously very distressed and demanding to be "forgiven" because the night before she had gone out with an older and married man she had met some days before while drinking at a nightclub. The nature of her anxiety was understood as a transferential acting out some sessions later, as we discovered that an angry part of the self had induced the acting and that now she was afraid mostly for two reasons: (1) The "opening" observed in the previous dream was a manipulation from the narcissistic gang to perpetrate internal control of the good parts of the self, guided by a revengeful hope to avoid separation anxiety. Going out with the married man also had the purpose of profaning the goodness of the analytical breast, allowing the narcissistic gang to deny the impotence of a child part, thwarting control of the external object, and perverting the setting by placing the analyst, via projective identification, in a very difficult dilemma: if I interpret the acting out I am against it, but if I say nothing I am an accomplice. Her panic and great pressure to come at a different hour represented the need to certify that I (the object) was still alive and not angry at her, that through her acting out she had not destroyed me. (2) Her separation anxiety prevented her from distinguishing between an internal childhood desire to completely control and overpower the internal mother to fulfill the basic delusion, on one hand, and the actual reality she was now facing, on the other. In other words, she was not capable of discriminating "time confusion" according to transferential displacement, or "space confusion" following projective and introjective identifications that her married friend not only was completely different from me (space confusion from projective identification) but also from her own parents (time confusion due to transferential projection).

136

A dream followed shortly after: *There was a war. She hid herself in a house across the street from her own house. There was also a girlfriend and her son. She was playing with the child and suddenly there was no more war. She heard some shooting, and two men came inside searching the house. One of the men was the analyst. She hid but had the feeling that she could still be seen.*

Within the oneiric scenario there appears again the previous ambivalence and the never-ending inner struggle: at the beginning there is a war, but later there is none, and at the end there is a war again. Defenses such as repression and splitting seem to take place, as there is her house and another house plus another woman and a child, and she is continually hiding, although she can also be seen. Perhaps we could speculate at this level that "being seen" after she hides might signify again the possibility of an opening, similar to the feeling of being "heard" in the dream of the tunnel. A few days after, she shared a perverse desire to control the object, together with a scopophilic phantasy: "I would like to see you while you observe me, but without you knowing that I am watching you." She waited and then said: "I don't think that you have said everything about me. I have read elsewhere about psychoanalysis, of an analyst who said to his female patient that he felt attracted to her, but that he wouldn't give in because such feelings were dangerous for the continuity of the analysis. I would like it if you were to feel the same way."

I said to her something like this: that the "internal gang" had convinced the "working part" of her that I was either her enemy and she couldn't trust me, or she ought to seduce me in order to control me, but in any case, we could not have a good analytical relationship; although there was also sometimes an opening, that the working part and I together could overcome those threats from the gang, and then either hear something or find something hidden. At the next session several memories appeared: She remembered, when she was little, how her parents had used her like a messenger between them when there were angry at each other; however, if the patient tried to complain, the mother usually inverted the situation by playing the role of the victim. She cried and managed to paralyze the patient with anxiety and remorse. Later on during the same session she remembered that when she was around 7 years old, she was in her bed masturbating her brother when the door opened and her mother appeared, screaming and hitting her. She also suspected that at a later age, between 8 and 9, a little neighbor boy was forbidden by his mother to play with her, perhaps for a similar reason.

I then noticed that the transference had taken a similar direction. She had dreams as well as fantasies where she was masturbating someone, a man, and at other times, more openly the analyst also. My interpretations and her continued denial, rejection, attack, or ignorance gave the impression of a mutual masturbation, where the relation was reversed: I would appear as her masturbating part and she as the masturbated innocent brother-neighbor. The analysis was also some kind of a game we were playing, an "as if" situation: if she did well, I would in the end participate in her masturbatory fantasies. A screen memory appeared shortly after: A maternal aunt, who was bathing her in the bathtub was also applying a cream to her vagina which felt very nice; however, she had another memory where the previous pleasant sensation changed into a painful one when the aunt introduced her finger inside her vagina.

Immediately after I came back from an Easter week holiday, she announced at the end of the session her decision to take the next week off. At the next session she expressed her fear that I might avenge myself because she was going away, although she denied that her fear of a vendetta could have been a projection associated with a retaliative acting out on her part, perhaps because she felt I had abandoned her before for one week. In the session immediately after her return, she remembered once when she had decided to change her job but was afraid that her working companions would reject her because she was leaving them; she feared I might do the same because she went away for a week. She didn't seem very pleased when I interpreted apprehension about me enviously attacking her, like she felt her friends at work might have done because she feared being discovered—or that she could also discover herself—that she was leaving them, excluding them, because she might have felt that they were no longer worthwhile. Two sessions later she brought the following dream: *I was traveling by car with my father, mother, and brother. I was trying to explain to my father my feelings about changing my work, but he did not understand. I felt very angry and I started screaming at him, calling him stupid several times, but he also got angry and slapped me in the face. I then stood up and got out of the car.*

This dream also represented the intense inner struggle between a superego part that stubbornly refused to understand (father part), and another part of the ego (herself) that was attempting to explain the presence inside of her of different libidinal as well as aggressive feelings: that she could have enjoyed leaving her job and going somewhere else, or taking a week's holiday; that by leaving her job or taking the week off she might have wanted to project onto the others a feeling of exclusion she wanted to get rid of; that she feared retaliatory feelings of envy that she had also projected; and finally, that she might use feelings of contempt to protect herself from a need of dependency.

I think the dream represented the inner struggle between a healthy aspect of the self that was continuously attempting to communicate (as in the previous dreams, being heard or being seen), and the tyranny of the bad objects, or the internal destructive and narcissistic gang. Such a tyranny interferes (either by threat and aggressive coercion, like a "slap in the face," or by "not understanding") with the purpose of maintaining the status quo ante, meaning, the control of the internal world and the predominance of primitive and infantile forms of object relations. The analysis "traveled" in a similar fashion to her "traveling" in the dream's car. "Not understanding" the interpretations constituted an immediate reflection of the internal scenario, now reproduced in the transferential interaction. The ego's failure to deal with the tyranny of the bad internal organization triggered the need for splitting-off mechanisms, represented at the end of the dream by her decision to get out of the car.

The interpretation following these last comments about the inner struggle between different parts of the self and so forth brought back a forgotten part of the dream that corroborated the hypothesis: Her brother (an ego part), who was sitting quietly next to her in the car, made a very interesting remark at the moment she was stepping out of the car, denouncing the repetition compulsion: "You are always escaping, you are always doing exactly the same."

One month later she arrived very anxious and was hesitant about telling a dream: *She was in the hospital where she worked, in the special unit for the treatment of brain-damaged children. The father of one of them was trying to take a picture of her and his child together. Then she was lying down on Dr. G.'s couch, the analyst of M., who like herself is also a psychologist and works in the hospital. He was next to the patient and opened his fly inviting her to make love to him. She tried to pull down her pants, but he stopped her and said not to do it but to perform fellatio instead.* She had no associations to the first part of the dream but became aware that Dr. G. bore a physical resemblance to her father. She then remembered that when she was little, her father used to kiss her while taking her to bed. She also recalled seeing M. sitting at the same table with Dr. G. during lunch, and thought that she could never do something like that with me.

It is possible to observe again the same inner struggle seen in previous dreams as well as in the transference during the analytical setting: on one hand, the desire of a healthy aspect of the self attempting to take a "picture" of the "organic" part, that is, the destructive narcissism, but immediately after there is the need to profane the goodness of the object, to change the purpose of the analysis as well as the fatherly kisses of her childhood. An interpretation offered along these lines brought the association of her relationship with a former boyfriend, who suffered from genital herpes and who also rejected her, making her feel that it was she and not he who was sick. I said to her that we were attempting, without too much success, to take a picture of an organic and envious aspect of herself that was continually trying to convince her that what her parents were giving to themselves was sick and not good; that such envious and poisonous attacks created also within herself such a feeling of uneasiness and guilt that to share the same table with her analyst-father was very dangerous, because another part of herself had convinced her internally that if she were discovered she could be poisoned. This made her very frightened.

Seven months later she referred to another dream: *She was an adolescent and there was a party at her house to celebrate her brother's birthday. Her mother was doing the necessary arrangements for the party. Suddenly the mother felt sick with a migraine, went to bed and disappeared; but then she was inside the freezer, cut into pieces that reminded her of one of Picasso's pictures. However, her mother was still talking and giving her advice about how to go on with the party.* She remembered that a similar situation occurred at her house when she was a child and an adolescent: "My mother would be telling me what to do; then she would have a migraine attack and go to her room, where she would continue giving instructions and mostly criticizing me, a situation that made me feel extremely unhappy." I then said to her that she felt trapped by a difficult dilemma: she wanted to destroy an internal mother who criticized and controlled her from within, but regardless of what she tried, this internal mother was still alive, and she felt hopeless because she feared it could remain "frozen" forever. The dilemma, on the other hand consisted of something else: if she destroyed the internal mother by "knowing" what to do and "taking over," she might be left completely alone; but if she was afraid to be by herself, she would have to preserve (freeze) the internal mother inside to tell her what to do and also to criticize her. Something similar was taking place in the analytical situation: if she didn't "know," she would have me forever—the analysis would freeze (negative therapeutic reaction); but if she became "aware," she would be able to leave.

The inner struggle continued determining the transference–countertransference dimension, the ambivalence between the need for inner destruction and the conscious desire to resolve her suffering: the need to fulfill the basic delusion of preserving forever (frozen) the inner image of a sick and invalid (migraine) mother, in pieces, to whom she would then be essential to "complete" her narcissistic fault.

Around one year later and after returning from a one-week holiday, she seemed very enthusiastic and mentioned that she did not feel anxious as she had in the past on similar occasions. She felt reliable, with better self-esteem, and for the first time, grateful for the analysis. In the phase of these changes I suspected three possibilities: a manic revenge: she had had a wonderful holiday and she did not need me any longer; she was trying to please me by giving me what she thought I needed; her feeling was genuine. She referred to a dream: *She was in a very wide bedroom with a big bed. There was a cabinet where she wanted to hide; but instead she decided to open it. Inside there were beautiful dresses, and she felt very exited and happy.* She associated this with her desire to eat more and gain weight so she would be able to wear several nice

143

dresses she had at home that were too big for her now. I said that now she felt her space was wider and unbounded, that although she feared to open the cabinet, she went ahead and did it, where she found her desire for a change— a new skin, a woman skin—and that she felt very happy about the possibility of such a change.

7

Borderline Structures and Mechanisms of Self-Envy

In his paper "Some Character Types Met With in Psycho-analytic Work" (1916), Freud described certain kinds of patients who "occasionally fall ill precisely when a deeply-rooted and long-cherished wish has come to fulfillment. It seems as though they were not able to tolerate their happiness; for there can be no question that there is a causal connection between their success and their falling ill" (p. 316). He concluded that "psycho-analytic work teaches that the forces of conscience which induce illness in consequence of success, instead of, as normally, in consequence of frustration, are closely connected with the Oedipus complex," (p. 331).

Although this continues to be true, it is possible, too, following Klein, that envy also plays a definite role in the intimate interaction between internal child and parental parts of the self in this kind of neurosis as well as in other types of patients I will describe further on. I am now referring to a form of self-envy in which envious child parts

147

of the self will internally attack and paralyze adult parts, parental-like or creative and sexually bounded objects.

In 1924 Freud based his concept of "moral masochism" on the effect of aggression directed against the self:

> It is very tempting, in explaining this attitude (of a moral and desexualized masochism), to leave the libido out of the account and to confine oneself to assuming that in this case the destructive instinct has been turned inward again and is now raging against the self; yet there must be some meaning in the fact that linguistic usage has not given up the connection between this norm of behavior and erotism and calls these self-injurers masochists too. . . . I pointed out the sign by which such people can be recognized (a "negative therapeutic reaction") and I did not conceal the fact that the strength of such an impulse constitutes one of the most serious resistances and the greatest danger to the success of our medical or educative aims. [1924b, pp. 165–166]

Referring to "masculine and feminine split-off elements," Winnicott (1951) mentioned the analysis of a patient who had introjected his mother's desire for him to be a girl as the existence within the self of a "pure feminine element" that out of envy did not allow the masculine part to feel free. Winnicott said to the patient:

> You feel as if you ought to be pleased that here was an interpretation of mine that has released masculine behavior. The girl that I was talking to, however, does not want the man released, and indeed she is not interested in him. What she wants is full acknowledgment of herself and over her own rights over your

body. Her penis envy especially includes envy of you
as a male. [p. 75]

But the concept of self-envy was originally introduced
by Clifford Scott in 1975 who saw it as a conflict between
depreciated and idealized aspects of the ego. Scott asks
why it is so difficult to speak about self-envy. If the
difficulty is one of imagining the internal world as a
complex combination of different parts and particles that
interact among themselves as well as with the external
world, then the ability to conceive self-envy may depend
simply on increasing the power of resolution of the psychoanalytic microscope by changing the objective from a
lower to a higher magnification.

Scott (1975) has also suggested intriguingly "that the
waking ego might envy the dreaming ego and break
the link, spoil the connection and have none of it—or,
at the most, only the memory of a token dream" (p. 336).
This type of self-envy interaction is more obvious in certain
types of borderline patients, very frequent among addicts,
who often show a very malignant and self-destructive
attitude that usually appears in the transference as a
negative therapeutic reaction. The complex nature of the
narcissistic organization of borderline patients has already
been discussed in the preceding chapter.

Self-envy implies the envious and destructive attack
that a narcissistic and destructive part of the self continuously exercises against the healthy and creative part of the
self, and the main importance of self-envy interpretation,
as I see it, consists in helping to emphasize the intrapsychic origin of the conflict, for three reasons: (1) It helps to
differentiate between inside and outside realities, which,

due to the intensity of projective and introjective identifications, are always so confused in narcissistic states. (2) It helps to locate the real source of the projection as a conflict that belongs to the inner world and not to the transferential mirage. (3) It also helps to organize the transferential interpretation, because on the one hand, this type of interpretation is indispensable to induce therapeutic regression and transferential neurosis, but on the other, it could also prompt confusion of a narcissistic nature between analyst and analysand. Interpretation is the instrument psychoanalysts use to induce psychic change. It is viewed by the destructive narcissistic organization as a danger that threatens the essence of its constitution. In this manner it will stubbornly oppose it. "Until such a narcissistic organization is dismantled and a rebellion against the tyranny of the bad part is mounted," stated Meltzer, "progress into the threshold of the depressive position is impossible.' " (1973, p. 106).

An important purpose of interpretation is to resolve time and space confusions, as they are continually distorted by transference and projective identification, respectively. When at a given moment interpretation is provided with the purpose of elaborating space confusion because of projective identifications, it will be very helpful to introduce awareness about the boundaries between internal and external spaces by also afterward interpreting self-envy. In my clinical experience, when this is done, there is usually a better understanding about the profile of unconscious phantasy on the part of both analyst and analysand. It helps the return of what is projected, diminishes the intensity of projective identification, and prompts the initiation of depressive mechanisms.

The relevance of this concept can be better understood if we take into consideration the statement introduced by Steiner (1981)

> that a perverse relationship may exist (between the healthy parts of the self and the destructive gang) and that the healthy part of the self may collude and allow itself to be knowingly taken over by the narcissistic gang. It is this quality which is externalized in the transference and gives rise to the perverse flavor of the interaction. . . . I have suggested that the patient's internal relationships are externalized in the transference and become manifest as a pressure on the analyst to enter into perverse collusion. [pp. 242–243]

Following this line of thinking, self-envy interpretations, by restructuring the boundary between internal and external spaces, not only will allow the analysand to bring the conflict back where it really belongs, within the limits of the self, helping to avoid the danger of perverse transferential collusion, but will also ease the transferential pressure exercised by powerful, aggressive, and perverse projective identifications. From a theoretical point of view, we may generalize by saying that interpretation ought to move from extratransferential grounds to transference and finally—as in the case of self-envy interpretation—to intrapsychic organization.

CASE 1

I will examine this theoretical concept with clinical material from the analysis of a 39-year-old single, attractive, and intelligent female patient—whom I will call Lidia—who complained about periods of anxiety or depression, suicidal ideas, and depersonalization. She had never before sought psychoanalytical help because she was "not convinced" it would work; for a short time she saw a therapist who used behavior modification techniques. She was a heavy smoker, drank regularly, and in her mid-twenties used illegal drugs such as acid, marijuana, and cocaine.

During her first session, she emphatically expressed her desire to be hypnotized in order to stop smoking. After approximately one year of analysis we identified a narcissistic gang of self-objects, led by a controlling part she referred to as the "diabolic one," whose main purpose was to exercise an anal sadistic attack and control of the object in order to avoid dependency as well as separation and annihilatory anxieties. Jealousy toward her younger sister, who she believed was favored by her father, was often an important source of pain. It was also a determining factor in choosing me as her analyst, something she rejected when it was suggested, at least during the first months of treatment. Transferential fantasies of an erotic nature soon surfaced, although they were more related to anal erotism, the need to turn the external object into one of the characters of her masturbatory phantasy, to stubbornly control, overpower, and obscurely denigrate the object to deal with her fear of separation, envy of the powerful breast, and threat from the presence of other siblings. There was a long history of repetitive relationships with men: first idealization and seduction, then denigration, omnipotent control, and slavery. She often stated, "I never break away completely from those men who had been my boyfriends. I think I like to use them, but I do not respect them." The transference took a similar course; the diabolic part got hold of the good parts of the self and enslaved them in order to approach and seduce the object, to coerce, manipulate, threaten, or use any other means available to subjugate and achieve a sadistic and powerful object control.

Although Lidia was a very attractive woman, her continual erotic manipulations induced countertransferentially a feeling more of cautiousness and concern than any sexual excitement or fantasy. The diabolic part pressured the analyst to enter into a narcissistic collusion, to form a destructive couple that would oppose and enviously attack the principles of the analytical contract, the genital creativity—the babies—of the harmonious parental couple.

The material I am about to present comes from a time a year after the analysis began. (The previous Friday we had talked about her envy, pain of exclusion from her father and her sister, and also her need for revenge.) It was a Monday session and she had stayed with a maternal aunt during that weekend. She stated that she was angry at herself because she felt like a child when the washing machine broke down after she put in some clothes to wash, and was afraid to tell her Aunt F. because she feared being scolded. Why was she afraid if, after all, it was a matter of money and she could easily find someone to fix it? she queried. Then she spoke about her difficulties in sharing some details. She felt shy talking about them, like they were bad words or like the indecent gestures usually performed by M. (another maternal aunt, mentally disturbed—"odd, unreliable, unpredictable, and very envious"—that she often talked about), who came to be included as one of her internal objects. She also found it difficult to insinuate herself with other men. After some hesitation, she then stated that what she found difficult to

153

tell me was that the washing machine broke down because a wire that accidentally came out of one of her bras fell inside and stopped it. At that level of her analysis she hesitated between an adult part of herself who could "fix" everything, and a child part who feared the need for complicity—she would not insinuate herself, but would prefer for me to do it—expecting "to stop" the psycho-analytical "machine" with her childlike exhibitionistic desires. The exhibitionistic-child part wishes for me to partner with her, to collude in order to attack and destroy—to stop—the analytical couple. It is also a struggle between the exhibitionistic-voyeur couple that wishes to enviously destroy both the analysand–analyst couple, a representation of the harmonious-parental couple she saw in her parents, as well as her father–sister couple. She also recalled that the other day when I left her session for a few minutes—my office is also in my house—it was because I went to see my wife, something that filled her with anger and envy; but she felt ashamed to tell me.

At the next session she brought a dream: *There were several children and there was the feeling that they had done something bad. She was nearby inside a car, and opened the door to let two children come inside, one in the front and the other in the back. She was not aware of their sex. As she drove away, the child behind attempted to poke the front door security knob with a wire.* It was a very special wire, like a surgical instrument. She perceived the car as herself, as well as the driver and the two children as internal objects. She remembered when she was a child and was driving along with her mother and sister in her mother's car. She was in the front when the back door suddenly opened and her sister fell out of the car as her

154

mother turned at one intersection. Her mother became aware of the accident only after a man who had picked up her sister from the road ran after the car, calling her. Although the patient witnessed the event, she could not say anything because she was in a state of shock. She insisted on the very special characteristics of the wire in the dream, as a "sophisticated surgical instrument."

I suggested that the "wire" that stopped the washing machine represented an envious and destructive part that was manipulated in such a manner as to project the guilt on the outside object; that she will not insinuate herself but will wait for the other to make the first move. This, I believe, represented the special aspect—surgical instrument—of the device. The purpose was not only to open the door and get rid of the rival (to clean the couch of any trace of her sister), to destroy the harmonious and loving couple, but also to project outside on the external object (to open the door), the guilt (will not insinuate herself) as an attempt to deceive the superego. Such a need to project, often seen in these cases, is responsible for the difficulty in observing more clearly mechanisms of self-envy: that the conflict is more between internal parts than a transferential interaction. In the dream, an adult–mother part of herself was driving the car, adult in the sense that it could fix anything or was also capable of an analytical working alliance. The child part sitting behind was manipulating in order to get rid of the other child part sitting in the front, but in a different order, because it was her sister sitting behind, the one that in her childhood memory fell out of the car. But in the dream the situation was inverted, signifying that now, at the present time, it is an excluded sister part of herself, the one who is attempting to destroy the harmonious

155

couple: the relationship between two parts of herself sitting in front of the car.

Cloacal confusion between anus and vagina is often observed in this kind of narcissistic organization, where the anus attempts not only to dirty the vagina but also to "rob" its function as a penis receptacle, as well as the orgastic place. A particular female patient referred to this type of dynamic as the "robber ass" ("culo ladrón").

A few days after the previous session Lidia brought the following dream: *She was walking with her mother, when suddenly she felt blood running down her legs because she was menstruating. Her mother brought her to a bathroom that was very dirty. The floor was filled with dirty water and it was very smelly. Her mother then washed her with clean water from the tap. Then she was in bed with a man who had overpowered her with the use of a hypnotic or something of that sort, and was introducing something like a rod into her anus. She woke up sexually excited.*

She remembered that she had had a similar experience of blood running down her legs when her menarche began, as well as some years later when she had to ask to use a bathroom in a shop nearby. She did not remember being upset on either occasion. The previous weekend, while returning from the beach, she decided to stop at a gas station, and while she was filling her gas tank, her girlfriend went to the bathroom and came back complaining bitterly about how dirty it was. Since Lidia was accustomed to traveling to all sorts of places, she thought she wouldn't mind using it, but her friend was right—it was absolutely impossible. After a long pause and obviously feeling rather upset, she "confessed" that the night before she was feeling anxious and could not fall sleep, so she decided to masturbate, something she will usually do by manipulating both her clitoris and her anus. She also stated that she often felt that the enjoyment induced by her anal manipulation dirtied the presence or the pleasure from her vagina. How could she explain, she asked, that she might prefer the use of her anus as a source of sexual pleasure, if she also had a vagina, exactly made by nature for such an act? Her diabolic side, she then answered, robbed her of her vaginal right to penetration, the right to a healthy and correct relationship. I then suggested that the difference perhaps remained in that the anus could dirty the penis, her father's penis, as an envious revenge against the genital couple, to avoid creativity, growth, or procreation, just as the "sinister" side might sabotage, break the analytical washing machine, or dirty the analytical working capacity. The dream, on the other hand, showed an ambiguous or ambivalent superego relationship, because a mother part led her to the dirty aspects of her sexuality, the anal envious narcissistic organization, but then also washed her with clear water.

CASE 2

Nancy was a 38-year-old married female professional and mother of four children, who came for treatment over three years ago for indefinite anxieties, bouts of depression, and difficulties in performing her work. A source of anxiety at that time was an extramarital relationship with a younger cousin. Very early in the analysis she referred to some childhood memories about being sexually caressed by her maternal grandfather and later, when she was around 6 years of age, by a man who visited her house often, a sort of gambler she referred to as the "card man," who used to entertain but who also fondled her sexually by putting his finger inside her vagina, holding her against his side while playing cards at the same time. As the analysis progressed, an internal object became the tough part of an envious, narcissistic, and destructive gang we came to name as the "card-girl and card-man" couple, which dominated and perverted the transference for a long time in a rather painful, difficult, stubborn, and obsessive manner. Very often she threatened to discontinue the analysis and used comments made by other therapists she knew who were friendlier with their patients, and who invited them to their houses, and so on. Other times she accused me of being too cold and distant, or she claimed that I unfairly decided all the rules and she had no other alternative but to confide, or she became openly and aggressively seductive. It became clear that there was a continuous struggle in her mind between an envious and destructive card-girl–card-man couple and a constructive and envied analysand–analyst couple, just as she might have felt about her parents or about the relationship between them and her younger siblings. For the last year she had been working on a historical investigation about the descendants of General X., a well-known father of independence. She had, however, delayed the publication so much over the sponsor's required time, either by senseless complaints to the publishers or by continually finding loose ends that she managed to identify but did not fix, that she came close to jeopardizing the whole project. Around this time she had some dreams clearly related to envious feelings about the high social position, wealth, and general sophistication of

General X.'s descendants. In one of them, she was attending a party given by the hero's great-granddaughter's daughter, who in reality had invited her several times for dinner in a very exclusive private club. The party in the dream, however, was taking place in such a poor section of the city that she was afraid she might be knifed. In another dream, *she was with several of her university friends around a working table, in the country house of General X.'s family. There were many papers on the table and they said, "Let's talk about battle S.," which was another piece of research she was working on. She wanted to stay, but a woman there said she must leave. She did not pay attention to the woman, who then grabbed her by the arm when she extended it (thus helping her) to drop a glass.* "It was like using the opportunity the lady was providing me when she got hold of my arm to let the glass fall. The glass broke in many pieces that flew everywhere, making a mess and creating a problem for everybody who was there."

There is a group from the university who are attempting to discuss a paper Nancy is now seriously working on in real life, representing—I believe—the creative aspects of the self. They are also staying at General X.'s relatives' country house, people she admires and envies because of their social position and vast wealth. At the same time there is an envious and excluded part who tries to boycott the meeting by breaking a glass and letting the pieces fly all over the place. The woman, I think, represents a healthy aspect of the ego that attempts to preserve the creative part by means of repression and dissociation—taking her out of the room—but is then manipulated by using her (ego) strength (the "opportunity'') for the purpose of a destructive boycott of the creative parts. A similar situation might also have been at work in Nancy's struggle to publish her book on General X.'s relatives.

The two sessions that follow took place right before the Christmas holidays, about four months after the previous material:[1]

Session A

PT: (Crying silently) I feel very sad. I don't know if it is because of the holidays and I won't be coming here, that tomorrow will be my last session and I will miss coming here. (Pause) And my husband and my daughters were fixing the Christmas tree and they were really enjoying themselves, but I felt outside, left out as if I didn't want to interfere. This is a moment to be embraced. (Crying) And it is difficult not to feel anxious, not to feel afraid, although I remembered that you once said that sadness doesn't necessarily have to kill you, and I thought that I would allow myself to feel more depressed now than I did before; before I wouldn't allow it to happen, I listened to music, dancing music, and I danced until I felt no sadness.

TH: (I felt a bit suspicious about her sadness; I didn't find it convincing enough. It took me a few minutes before I realized that she really was crying. I felt

---

[1]The material that follows (Sessions A and B) was previously published in the *International Journal of Psycho-Analysis*, (1992): 73:719–728, and is reprinted by permission of the Institute of Psycho-Analysis.

that there might be some manipulation, but I preferred not to say anything in order to avoid inducing feelings of persecution.) I said: "I wonder why so much sadness; after all, we will be separated only for a few days. I wonder if this separation is perhaps triggering other circumstances more relevant in your life?"

PT: The only thing I can think of is the death of my father; however, that is already more than a year and a half ago. Perhaps there are things from my childhood that I don't remember. Perhaps when my cousin Z. (her boyfriend) left . . .

TH: (While she was talking, my phantasy was that her sadness might have something to do with the card girl–card man, that perhaps she was sad because our separation meant some kind of hopelessness on the card-girl part, just as happened when Z. left. However, I said nothing and decided to wait.)

PT: (Continues) Yesterday the two maids who work in my house didn't come to work and I was washing the dishes, and while I was doing this I asked myself what I really want from you, and I thought that what I want is a nice relationship, something lasting, not just a sexual affair as I wanted before, but a nice loving relationship.

TH: I wonder if the threat of separation, like here between us or your couple of mother-maids who did not come to work, triggers inside of you the need from a part of you to sell you a relationship, different this time from before because it is perhaps more sophisticated, not only sex, but more idealistic. But the important thing about this, I think, is not that you want to establish this type of relationship with me; after all you are proposing nothing

161

out of the ordinary between a man and a woman. The problem, I think, is that if we were to go ahead and establish this kind of ideal relationship it would destroy your family as well as our analytical relation. It reminds me of Aesop's fable, I do not know if you know it, about the dog with the piece of meat . . .

PT: Yes, I do.

TH: . . . Well, you will let go two important and real relations in your life just for something that does not exist. Maybe this need to repeat, this desire, might stem from early memories, when you felt your parents loved each other as well as your brothers and sisters, but left you out, and perhaps you feel it might be happening now with us because of the holidays. I wonder if there is the wish of a part of you to destroy, out of envy, another part of you, the one that relates with your husband and daughters, like your parents did, or the analytical couple, as if an excluded part of you feels very envious of the part of you that couples with your family and with me.

PT: Could be, after all my daughters are big now and we relate very freely, like I did with my brothers and sisters, just as if we were four sisters, and my husband is very generous with them and with me. They could represent my own family. And I am aware that very often when they are doing something together, like the Christmas tree, I feel left out, as if I don't belong there.

Session B

The next session was the last before the holidays and immediately after the previous one.

PT: I saw a lady coming out of your house and she was smiling as if she was very happy, and it is the first time that I saw someone coming out of here; usually it is very solitary around here. This morning I had a dream: *I was at the university writing my exam for my master's, which consisted of making crêpes, but it was very weird because I was making them with cotton wool, and I was taking out the seeds and wrapping them in banana leaves like a hallaca.[2] One was left there on the table, and somebody wrapped it up with a napkin and hooked it on a dry branch or something of that sort.* I woke up and went to eat some cookies, when two of my daughters arrived from a party, it was around two-thirty in the morning. I went to bed and lay down next to my husband. With one hand I was touching his hair, and I slipped the other down and I started softly touching his genitals to see if he responded. I thought that I would like to get hold of you in the same manner, half asleep. Then I fell sleep again and had another dream: *I was walking with a friend, someone with whom I went to Mexico. It was the downtown area of some city. Then I saw a piece of ham on the floor. I don't remember anything else.* About the other dream, the cotton reminds me of the first time when I saw a cotton plant. I was a child and I thought that it was very strange, different, very neat, a flower that didn't have any petals and that could be used as it was, without any change, to make clothes. I also remembered several years ago when a friend invited me to go to an island in

---

[2]Very popular Venezuelan tamale (dish of seasoned minced meat and maize), specifically made around Christmas time.

the middle of the Orinoco River. It was an island that disappears completely during certain times of the year because the river floods. There was a cotton plantation, and the plants were half submerged and had marks of previous floods around the trunk, and there were also many lagoons that remained after the waters retired, filled with piranhas and alligators, which we fished for food. That island was marvelous, like magic.

TH: (The previous week she had expressed her desire to bring me some *hallacas* she had cooked herself as a gift, something customary among friends and relatives, which she had never expressed previously. I thought that in her dreams she was referring again to the same phantasy, and it was this incident, I think, that induced me to say something at that particular moment. Although I felt there was a lot of material, I decided to insist just on her need to pervert the transference, to seduce in order to control, to deceive, leaving out, for instance, the last part of the first dream about the crêpe that was hooked on a dry branch, or the second dream, which could have been perhaps another "gift.") I said: "Maybe there is something else wrapped in the *tamales* you wish to give to me, something like a magic wish that could change me into the card girl and allow you to perform your phantasy of masturbating me like the card man did to you, and then you might smile just as you felt the other person who was here before you did."

PT: You could be right, although I don't like this thing of deceiving. I like cooking and I like to do it well, to experiment and invite people for dinner. I trained my cook to do the same, to surprise us with different sauces, and the people who come over love to eat at my house. I don't like what you have said about the card girl, that I am trying to do the same thing again; in any case it is your opinion, and since you are always giving your opinion, I don't know if it is right.

TH: Well, and what about you giving your own opinion

PT: I don't know, perhaps you are right and I just don't like it to be always the same.

TH: Perhaps there is a part of you, inside of you, that wishes to train us both like you have done with your cook, and to do it in such a way that we will be always doing the same but without knowing it, because we will be feeding each other with something that might appear different, but underneath it is exactly the same old card-girl–card-man type of relationship. And you said that you didn't like deceiving, and I wonder if what you might dislike is not so much deceiving me, but that a part of you has managed to deceive you, because what might exist underneath, submerged, is not so much a little girl who wants a man to masturbate her, but a little girl who would like to have a nice and resourceful mother who continually feeds her, that the need might be more from a hungry mouth than from a hungry vagina.

Comments about the Sessions

I believe that this patient is less anxious now, compared with how she presented at her first visit, perhaps because she has learned, since then, about the close link between

165

her need to fulfill childhood fantasies (card girl-card man) with the purpose of controlling and attacking the object out of revenge, and the level of guilt and persecutory anxiety that the need to fulfill such phantasy will always elicit as a complication. I chose the first of the two sessions before the Christmas holidays because I felt mechanisms of self-envy were more evident in it, and the second session because I wanted to see what sort of inference, if any, the dynamics that took place during the previous session might have on the unconscious phantasy. There were many other avenues I might have chosen; however, I kept the interpretations oriented toward her need to pervert the transference and the mechanisms of self-envy, because I felt these were the main sources of her internal suffering.

CASE 3

Claire was a young, attractive French-Canadian woman, the older of two sisters, married for six years and mother of one boy by the time of her divorce. She was working as an interior decorator when she consulted, because she felt very unhappy about her marital difficulties, thought that her husband X. was very selfish, and suspected also that he might have been unfaithful, although she had no proof of it. At the same time she felt very apprehensive about confronting him openly, and this inhibition made her very angry at herself.

She had married against her parents' advice; her father never liked or trusted her husband because he was an artist, rather bohemian, unreliable, and a poor provider.

166

Although there were obviously some difficulties in communication, it seemed to me (countertransference) that the differences between Claire and X. could have been worked out. She then got herself sexually involved with D., a mutual friend, three times divorced and now separated from his wife. When she told her parents about her affair with D., they were again very much against it, often expressing their concern because they felt that D. was even worse than X. Finally she separated from X., and now she feels more free and less guilty about her relationship with D.

Although the situation was often examined in the analysis as a form of a transferential acting out, nothing changed her determination to go ahead with her divorce as well as her emotional involvement with D. Countertransferentially, I began to suspect a need for revenge after having been excluded (present in her own marriage, and perhaps related to the birth and presence of her younger sister), which could have been decided around an oedipal retaliation against her own father, and was now being repeated with her husband and her boyfriend. Within the analytical setting any reference about such revenge was either ignored or strongly denied, and for quite some time it was mostly the analyst's theory. Usually after my interpretation of this subject, she kept a protective silence and subsequently either would not mention anything about it once she resumed her discourse, or would ask questions, giving the impression that she was ignorant about such matters and since it was my own theory, I should have all the answers: "Why a revenge? How did it happen? What will come next? What do you think?" and so on.

At one point, Claire started the session referring to a movie in which an old Italian man's children, adults

167

already, do all sorts of things to deceive their father, lying about their professions and style of living. One of his daughters, for instance, already separated from her husband, asks him to move back in again with her during the time of her father's visit. Then Claire said that her mother, who was overseas for a while, had returned and brought presents for everybody but X. Although Claire was aware of the repercussions such an insult might produce in her already troubled marriage, she could not say anything to her mother: "It was stronger than me." I told her that she wanted to project onto me a deceived component, resembling the old Italian man's role, in order for me and for an equal part in her not to see that there was also another component in her, similar to her mother's attitude, which was trying simultaneously to attack and destroy the harmony in her family by introducing a sense of exclusion. The power of this need was so strong that she could not do anything—it was stronger than she was.

As the analysis continued, the existence of several internal objects constituting at least three main elements became more apparent: (1) a sadistic component, primitive and stubborn, guided by a revengeful hope that followed the all-or-nothing slogan: it was absolutely that revenge or nothing at all; (2) a naïve, beguiled, deceived element (like the old Italian man); (3) a manipulator-saboteur that deceived, lied, disguised, and continually attempted to get control of the ego in order to change it and maintain it as a naïve-deceived-element (element 2). Frequently the discourse was controlled by element 3.

She usually mentioned how right she felt in not wanting to improve her relationship with her husband because, after all, he had treated her so terribly. I got the impression that she was not only trying to convince herself, but also attempting to make me her accomplice in the process of denying the guilt caused by the hate against her husband and by the need to have a lover. I was the repository of a projective identification configured according to element 2, that is, naïve and deceived. Interpretations attempting to restore the projection were received with silence, after which she either asked questions about what I said, as if it was just my theory, or kept on talking as if I had said nothing.

Around this time something extremely interesting started to take place. The regular routine followed the dynamics I have just described, until she started to bring dreams that seemed to portray a more truthful view of what was really taking place. While she was attempting to convince both herself and the analyst, with the help of the manipulator–saboteur element, that everything was fine, another part of herself was denouncing her by means of her dreaming activity. This, for instance, is a typical dream: *"I was staying at my Uncle André's place, when someone telephoned and said that a terrible crime had been committed at my place, that my husband X. had been killed. But they used D.'s name [her boyfriend] instead of my husband's name. I went there and found that it was not D. who was dead but X., but then it was both of them, X. and D."* Uncle André, a maternal uncle, was described as a nice, very loving, and understanding person. When she was going to marry her husband X. and her father was so much against him, her uncle was the only one who made X. feel welcome. I thought that Uncle André represented a naïve accomplice who was at that time "deceived" and who could not see the potential crime then taking place: the desire of an envious part of herself that wanted to destroy by means of revenge her father, by getting married without his consent; her husband, now as a father representation, once she got involved with D.; her analyst, when she refused to acknowledge the interpretations.

The real crime, of course, was against the possibility of creating a harmonious couple, a good, understanding, and faithful marriage. Something that was impossible for her to produce at this point, because the possibility of a loving marriage as she felt existed between her parents when she was a child or between them and her sister, used to be and still is so threatening, and induced such anger and envy, that she was compelled to destroy it repeatedly. This occurred mostly out of envy against the inner self-object, which represented the loving parental couple: her own desire for a harmonious, loving, faithful relationship.

The transcription of an entire session follows. By this time she was in her third year of analytical treatment, four times weekly, and had already been separated from her husband for at least six months. This was a Monday session.

PT: I had a dream. *I dreamed about a model of a house made by D., my boyfriend, who is an architect. It was made of metal, which is how he usually builds his models. And there was a very pretty facade, and on top of it there were three wooden heads. Suddenly one of the heads fell down and I tried to pick it up, but then D. took it from my hand and put it back again. However, I knew that it was going to fall again. The three heads*

170

had nothing to do with the facade; they were made of wood, of a different material from the rest of the model. And when I picked it up—the head that fell—it was very light, not like the heavy metal the model was made of. D. always makes his models with very heavy metals. (Pause)

D. was telling me yesterday that someone came to his house and told him that there was an apartment for sale in the same building where my parents live, that he was very tired of living by himself, and that he would like for me to live with him. Of course, this is very different from what he said before, that we should take our time, not to rush, not to get too involved so soon. And I told him that he was crazy, that I wouldn't like to move to a place where everybody knew me and I would have to hide all the time. . . . I think that the heads might represent the three apartments in the same building: my parents are living in one, my sister is planning to move to another, and now D. is trying to buy one.

TH: (I felt that perhaps there was a contrast between what I felt the dream was expressing and her own associations. I thought that element 3 was again trying to hide the evidence. It made more sense to me that the three heads represented her marriage, and that perhaps she was portrayed by the fallen one.) I wonder if you have thought that the heads could also have been related to your marriage?

PT: Could be, and the head that fell down might represent X. Now that I think of it, the other two heads were together, attached to each other and could not fall down. N. (her son) enjoys playing a lot with X. And I have been rather angry lately because X. says that he is very busy at the moment and cannot stay with N. as long as he should, because he is working too hard and he doesn't like to do it just for a short time because that might frustrate both the child and himself. He asked me if I could bring N. to his office, and that infuriated me, that he could ask me that, but then I thought that usually the children are the ones who suffer more in a divorce. I calmed myself down and felt that I should take N. to see his father. And the heads were very light and hollow, very thin, perhaps that might represent the amount of love left between X. and myself.

TH: What about if we were to think that the head that fell down was your own?

PT: That could be too, and the two heads that didn't fall off and were together were X. and N. And it was D. who in the dream helped me to lift the fallen head and to put it back.

TH: (I thought that I—the analyst—was suggesting that the fallen one was hers and not her husband's, that again, it was my theory and not hers, that there was a contrast between her associations and what I thought the dream might have represented, and that possibly she was accepting my suggestions not because she really believed them but perhaps because she was trying to pacify me. I didn't say anything at this moment.)

PT: (Long pause) My sister is moving and wants to sell all her furniture, and I knew that D. needed furniture for his wife's apartment because he is now living by himself, so I mentioned to him about buying my sister's furniture. I told my father about it and he said that it was okay, that if D. didn't have any money now he could pay it in two or three months. This is very, very strange; my dad is against D. and now he appears so generous. He was not like that at all with X.

TH: And now he seems to be an accomplice, and perhaps you feel that I am not, that I insist on making you see things in a different way.

PT: (Interrupting) That's right.

TH: (I thought that an important element in her was sure that the real problem was that I was not convinced—*convinceable*, would have been the right word—as her father was, that if I were to be convinced, then everything would be all right. She was attempting a transferential collusion with the analyst as a way to avoid becoming aware that the conflict was between two different elements inside of her. I felt that it was important to demonstrate this.) I continued: "It seems to me that there is this element that I have referred to before that is trying to convince us that there is nothing to worry about, either about your divorce or about your relationship with D., while at the same time there seems to exist another part of you, very often present in your dreams, that attempts to show otherwise; that it could have been your own head that fell from your marriage and that now it does not fit inside D.'s facade, inside D.'s life, even if he tries to "help" by insisting on provoking your father by living together in the same building. However, you are not sure if now your dad might have changed, like your Uncle André, into another accomplice, and perhaps you feel now that I take sides with the dreaming side of you and insist on pointing out how the stubborn part of you persists in attempting a relationship where your head might fall again. As if a part of you is convinced and is also trying to convince me that it is fine for your head to keep falling off and obstinately obstruct or destroy out of envy another part of you that could fit properly in a loving and lasting relationship that you might deserve.

PT: (Pause) My mother once said, when I was an adolescent, that all boys I had relationships with were shit, that there was something about me that attracted shit. Perhaps, like you said, I am now doing the same thing I did with X. when I married him, and D. is another shit. But even if I try to convince myself I cannot; it is something stronger than me. I am convinced that this is a very nice and loving relationship and I am not capable of changing it otherwise.

CASE 4

Duncan was a 47-year-old married male with three children, a heavy drinker and smoker, who consulted five years ago because of anxiety, sexual impotence, and marital difficulties. He had a younger sister. He was sort of a chronic complainer, in a negative therapeutic reaction fashion, never pleased with himself, his work, his family, or the analysis. Through the years we had examined several avenues: a masochistic need for punishment, fear of retaliation from enviously destroyed objects, a defense against castration anxiety by deceiving the possible castrator—"See how miserable I feel"—or even more, the desire to find someone he might convince to adopt him in

174

order to take revenge later, and so on. Lately we had been working on his rivalry with his sister, who he felt was favored by his father and, according to him, was always right and very successful in her marriage, work, and family. I had previously suggested that "all" feelings of well-being belonged to his sister, that there were two parts inside of him: a chronic complainer part, whose main purpose was to destroy out of envy any possibility of enjoyment in him as well as in others—including the analyst—and another part, the "joyful one," which he felt belonged solely to his sister and which he attacked and destroyed most, not only in others—via projective identification—but within himself, as if his own feelings of well-being were not his, but his sister's.

Around this time he started a session referring to an important meeting he was going to attend that day. Jack, his business associate, was abroad, and Duncan was afraid that the people he was going to meet might take away a line of importation he and Jack had neglected. He felt optimistic, however. He was going to do things his way, without having to wait for Jack or consult him either, as he used to do before. He felt much better, but he was aware of how difficult it was for him to talk freely about it. It was easier to complain when he felt bad than to talk when he felt good. Then I said that it seemed that his feeling of well-being was illegal. After a short pause he remembered a dream: *He was someplace talking amicably with Jack, when suddenly Jack's face changed and he became very angry and aggressive. Then Jack complained that he was very angry with him because of what he did to Anna.* After awakening he became aware that Anna was in reality Jack's sister, something he associated with his own

175

sister—how his father, when Duncan was a child, used to complain about him bothering her.

Jack was a part of himself complaining about the way he treated his inner-sister part, how he would attack "her" by destroying within himself his own feelings of well-being, while at the same time also destroying her within the others by means of projective identification: his chronic complaints not only sheltered the purpose of making any feeling of well-being illegal, but also covered up his continuous envious attacks on his inner-sister "well-being" part. At this session he was also expressing his desire to do things his way, meaning, perhaps, to save the line of work he had neglected, to face the Jack inner-part saboteur, to separate his own feeling of well-being from his sister's, and to legalize his own right for enjoyment. She was, as he himself put it, a Siamese-twin ghost attached to himself by envy that he wanted, most anxiously, to be rid of.

SELF-ENVY AND ACTING OUT

In some borderline patients, of the kind I have described here, one frequently observes a significant tendency to use acting out as a form of aggressive and destructive communication. An "as if," complying facade hides a destructive and negativistic aspect of the self that enviously attacks idealized aspects projected in the outside object. In the analysis of these patients, the transference is determined by both a compliant and obsequious tendency to establish a "perfect analytical couple," and a need to institute a "revengeful couple" that surfaces once the patient has met the demands the analytical setting is presumed to impose: free association, lying on the couch, and so on. Between these two strong possibilities, to comply and to destroy, struggles a fragile and incipient ego attempting to gain recognition, mastery, and autonomy over the whole personality but instead, it is completely subjugated and manipulated by the powerful narcissistic gang. The beginning of the analysis is completely dominated by the presence of the perfect analytical couple; everything is absolutely fine, the patient associates and brings important material to the sessions, the analyst is pleased about the interpretations, and everything seems to run smoothly, when suddenly, like lightning out of a blue sky, appears, incomprehensibly, the acting out.

The perfect couple represents the continuous reproduction by imitation of an idealized, loving, and harmonious couple, constituted in the past by both parents, or by them and other siblings, watched and introjected by the patient who feels painfully excluded. This scenario, repeated over the years as a consequence of an infinitude of conditions, induces in these patients the feeling that any harmonious and loving relationship exercised by others and even by the patients themselves represents, as in the past, a state of being that belongs to the "enemy," to others, but never to the patients: it is foreign stuff to which they have no access and never will. However, at the same time they cannot escape the fatalism of a repetition compulsion, the need to reproduce the same harmonious interaction they once saw and envied during early life. The perfect couple represents the condensation of several layers of identification, among them: the harmonious couple once observed in others, a way of complying to please a castrator, and a re-creation by imitation of what is envied. However, the re-creation of the perfect couple in the transference also seems to trigger the envied excluded element, exactly as in the past.

While the perfect couple represents the good but foreign aspects of the self, the "excluded element" constitutes the need to attack and destroy such good elements by means of acting out, that is, the need to provide others with exactly the opposite of what the patient feels others want; this is the motivation that propels the acting out. I can think of several cases of this kind:

Christine was a 32-year-old medical doctor, married with three children, the only child of parents divorced when she was about 5 years old. She came for consultation due to chronic anxiety, depressive states, and heavy drinking. Her mother was also an alcoholic, as was her father, and she grew up as the poor rich child in a severely emotionally deprived environment, raised mostly by maids, and seeing very little of her mother. After three years of analysis, she has managed to keep her marriage together, maintain a steady job, and give birth to two children. However, several months ago, on a Sunday afternoon, she started to drink again in the same way she did before coming for analysis. The next Monday she was very apologetic: "I am sorry, I didn't mean to hurt you," and so on, as if she felt that she had really done something bad to others, but not to herself. It was the dynamic of a false self, where only others existed, since she had done more damage to herself than to anybody else. The existence of a narcissistic, envious, and destructive gang then became clear; she was trying to attack and destroy the perfect couple that had developed during those three years of treatment; a pseudo-analysis had obscured this revengeful, envious element, which remained unchanged but surfaced now when everything appeared to be much better than before. This polarization of split parts, between a need to comply and a need for revenge, is used as a defense to avoid the appearance of the depressive state necessary to undertake any work or reparation.

Michael was another case, a 30-year-old homosexual, the only boy and youngest of four siblings, who grew up without the presence of a father, exposed to the "penis envy" of four women. He experienced the contradiction of two opposite forces: he was both excessively overprotected by his family, to the point of degradation, and very much expected to fill the place left by an absent father and husband. Throughout his life he reacted with dissociation between a social and submissive part that continually tried to please, and the need to act out as an illegal, very destructive, and corrupt (homosexual) element that incessantly attempted to undermine any ego-ideal expectations. There was a great amount of persecutory anxiety linked to his homosexual activity (acting out), usually carried out in a casual, destructive manner under the influence of cocaine and without any precautions against venereal diseases, including HIV. He was brought in for consultation by his older sister after being arrested by a police undercover agent for attempting to buy cocaine. His great fear was that his relatives would find out that he was a homosexual, although we managed to clarify later in the treatment that his concern was really more related to his family knowing about his destructive envious attack against their heterosexual expectations. Although he was not particularly mannered or effeminate, he preferred passive homo-

179

sexual relations where he reached orgasm by anal penetration only, without having to masturbate. He searched for sexual partners in heterosexual bars, hoping to find bisexual men. He also understood that his drug abuse was a superego manipulation related to the need to "not be there" while he was having a homosexual affair: he did not want to know about it.

Approximately one year after the treatment commenced, he started to complain about feelings of loneliness, of how difficult it was for him to face the fact that he was not going to have a family of his own. He had a dream: *He was walking at night in a dark street downtown, when suddenly a man appeared, tall and dark with a hat and dressed in blue. The man was carrying a machine gun and was shooting at people. The patient managed to hide, and the man passed without seeing him. Afterward, the patient saw many dead people. They were mostly young, heterosexual couples.* In his associations he recalled feeling very anxious when his mother inquired when he was going to get married. Afterward, he sensed his mother's intrusion and got angry. The man of the dream he associated with a black friend who is married and has children but who also has a homosexual relationship with him. He admires him a great deal because he is capable of both kinds of relationships. He remembered what I said during the previous session, how his passive homosexual role could be related to an unconscious envious desire to dirty men's penises in order to make them useless. The blue color of the man's outfit reminded him of some kind of sailor's suit that his mother forced him to wear when he was a child and that he despised. About the dead couples he could provide no association, but he recalled a nice girl who works near his office and who seems to like him, because she is often making suggestions about going out, something he feels very frightened of.

I thought that the black man represented an envious component that continually attacked within the self the heterosexual part (young couples), mostly his own penis, which he renders ineffective during his homosexual relations. Heterosexuality is part of the ego ideal, related to the desire of his internal parents, which he also wants to attack and destroy. In other words, he attacks within himself exactly what he admires. He had a great deal of persecutory anxiety in the form of castration anxiety, a condition that induces a tendency toward a corruption of transference, and he feels trapped between a powerful need to create a homosexual collusion with the analyst and the panic of a possible heterosexual demand.

8

Self-Envy and Intrapsychic Interpretation

THE THREE PHASES OF INTERPRETATION

Psychoanalysis has considered two probable areas of interest and investigation in constructing interpretation: (1) hypothesizing about the analysand's relationship, either genetically or with others outside the analytical setting, that is, *extratransference interpretation;* (2) following interchange of projective and introjective identifications within the transference, or *transference interpretation.* Without succumbing to the arguments for privileging one viewpoint over the other that have induced psychoanalysts over the years to take sides, I would like to consider special clinical circumstances encountered in borderline patients with distinct paranoid or perverse traits, where transference interpretations could induce complications or a dangerous collusion that might increase resistance instead of working through—a condition perhaps where neither the

185

extratransference nor the transference interpretation is the best solution to ease the pain of mental suffering, because either might—as I said—facilitate the progress of a trans-ference perversion. We might consider instead the possi-bility of directing the interpretation toward the inner interaction of part self-objects inside the self, attempting to clarify the intimate and complex interplay of different self-parts and self-objects within the boundaries of the inner self. While extratransference interpretation, as Gill (1982) has stated, leaves out the possibility of dealing directly in the here and now with the transference of emotional projective identifications, transference interpre-tation brings about in these patients the danger of a transference collusion, a perversion of transference, and immediate clinical complications. *Intrapsychic interpreta-tion*, or interpretation about the conflict between the parts, allows the conflict to be brought to the realm of the inner world, where it really belongs, to show that the true conflictive interaction happens between different intro-jects within the self, and not in the reflection of the transference mirage. Transference collusion is usually the consequence of persecutory anxiety induced by objects projected in the analyst via projective identification, re-quiring the analyst's presence in order to control the persecutory anxiety. In other words, the main purpose of the transference collusion is a desperate attempt to deal with the failure of a projection used as a defense to free the self from a persecutory object, having to resort, because of this failure, to give substance to the projected object in the presence of the analyst. There are at least two kinds of borderline patients who might resort to mechanisms of transference collusion: either paranoid structures or perverse pathology.

Steiner (1981) has denounced, in a patient similar to those I am describing here, the presence of a perverse interaction between different part objects within the self:

> He [the patient] invited interpretations but in such a way that, if I responded, it produced an uneasy feeling that I had been drawn into an activity which might resemble analysis but was futile and irrelevant to his actual needs. . . . I have suggested that the patient's internal relationships are externalized in the transference and become manifest as a pressure on the analyst to enter into perverse collusion. They are also, however, discernible in the patient's dreams, associations, and fantasy life, and these often help the analyst to understand what is going on and help him to avoid acting out with the patient. [pp. 241, 243]

We have already seen this narcissistic organization in Chapter 4, where, following Rosenfeld's contributions (1971), I described the existence of an internal association of bad destructive elements, similar to the organization of a "gang Mafioso," whose main purpose will be to control the good aspects of the self by exercising a tyranny by means of threat, coercion, manipulation, seduction, deceit, and so on. For instance, this internal gang might convince a patient's ego that the best way to avoid castration would be to provide to the other as a potential castrator, exactly what the patient feels this castrator might wish, inducing in this fashion, a continuous, exhausting, manic, chameleonic, or "as-if" behavior in order to comply with the other's demand. This type of patient will manufacture anything, including the posture of the "ideal" analysand, effecting a false analysis. But this need to comply will induce the fear of an identity diffusion, fear that the dependent parts of the self could be hurt, generating at the same time, as a defense, a great amount of envy, frequently hidden in the form of a secret weapon, often of anal sadistic character, concealed in the feces or the anus, where no one would ever imagine it, with the main purpose of undermining the object's goodness as well as any kind of link (Bion 1959) with it, and to attack and destroy all of this with pleasure. The narcissistic gang may also deceive and convince the ego of that negative identification—that is, revenge, acting out, idealization of "badness," and profanation and denigration of "goodness." There is an endless circularity, a pathological equilibrium established according to a pattern, in which the greater the need to comply in order to avoid castration, the greater the need to enviously attack and destroy, and, as a consequence, the greater the need to comply, and so forth.

In other patients, castration anxiety might induce a different solution, for instance, the need to reestablish the old symbiotic tie with the mother. The narcissistic organization in this kind of borderline patient will also have a perverse feature, usually built around a powerful force, guided by hope based on revenge, that conditions the purpose of the ego and determines the outcome of behavior. Such revenge, of which the Count of Monte Cristo is a paradigm, is directed against parental objects incorporated within the self. Behind the revenge is a disavowal of early emotional pain from oedipal exclusion and castration anxiety, both provoked by the threat of maternal symbiosis breaking up. Among these patients is the common belief that they are essential in order to complete the maternal narcissistic fault, or the absence of a penis, an unconscious phantasy always sustained by the mother's unresolved penis envy. The child builds this belief as a basic delusion, as I have stated previously (López-Corvo 1990, 1992), of being absolutely indispensable for the mother's completeness, as a form of mitigation for the pain induced by the change from a dualistic narcissism (symbiosis) to an oedipal triangulation, as well as the creation, consequently, of a painful space for exclusion. If this suffering reaches very painful levels, the child will disavow the mother's completeness by creating the basic delusion that if he (or she) is not fulfilling the mother's absence, it is not because the mother is autonomous and does not require it but because someone else is doing it. To avoid terrible hopelessness and despair produced by reality (i.e., that the mother is autonomous), these patients prefer the envy, anger, and feeling of revenge induced by their delusion. This may be the first suspiciousness that appears in human beings. The revengeful hope is based on the belief that the rival can be destroyed and the original symbiosis with the mother will again be restored forever. The mother's completeness or autonomy is never accepted by the internal child of these patients, because such a doubt will elicit the fear that castration is possible; what is challenged by them is the fact that somebody else (father, other siblings) has replaced them. Revenge then, against the usurpers, will be sold to the ego as the only possible hope against suffering. Anything that links—love, happy couple interactions, family harmony, and soon—will elicit very painful feelings of envy, always creating the impression that such a scenario is unattainable for them or for the excluded part of them. Once they have grown and developed as well as exercised some of these links themselves, the excluded part within the self will enviously attack the harmonious part that is now being exercised; in other words, self-envy will materialize.

Transference in these patients acquires a very particular characteristic because of the need to induce by means of intrusive projective identifications a perverse relationship with the analyst, a transference collusion or resistance with the purpose of establishing a revengeful couple, parallel, hidden, and illegal, solely guided by the perverse purpose of establishing a fantasied status quo ante. This perverse and illegal couple runs parallel to an "as-if" or pseudo-analysis, which the patient will willingly engage in as compliance with the "peculiar" demands made by the analyst (lying down on the couch, free association, etc.); sometime later, if the patient goes along with it, he or she will be "rewarded," once the revengeful couple is finally established, a mechanism to which we have been alerted by Meltzer (1973), Joseph (1975), and Steiner (1981), among many others. The presence of this perverse couple is experienced as a transference pressure to establish a more personal relationship with the analyst: sitting up or turning around to see the analyst, asking direct questions, bursting into narcissistic rage if the existence of the revengeful couple is threatened, complaining about the analyst's neutrality, and so on. There are other general characteristics, such as the need to be unique, to be an exception, as Freud (1916), Kris (1976), and more recently Ladan (1992) have described. Another aspect is the necessity to project a helpless aspect of the self, which will create the omnipotent illusion of a fragile, nonautonomous, and incomplete analyst-mother, who will require of the patient continuous assistance: the patient comes to analysis not because he or she is in need of help but to look after the analyst. In these cases, the transference interpretation could become, paradoxically, a dangerous formula capable of inducing further transferential narcissistic collusion, instead of neutralizing anxiety and mobilizing defenses toward a more depressive state.

The interpretation is the instrument used by the analyst to induce psychic change; this is why the interpretation will be sensed as a threat by the revengeful couple, which will stubbornly oppose, with very powerful resistance, any possible change (Rosenfeld 1971). It is only after this narcissistic, envious, and revengeful organization is denounced with the help of the observing ego, and the tyranny over the weak ego abrogated, that the process toward a depressive position becomes possible (Meltzer 1973).

A very important aspect of all interpretations is the intention to resolve the confusions of time as well as of space, because both dimensions have been distorted by the effect of transference and projective identification, respectively. When interpretation is carried out with the purpose of resolving spatial confusion induced by powerful projective identification (returning the projected), it is useful in these cases to introduce also awareness about outer and inner limits with the use of intrapsychic interpretation. The real substance of the unconscious phantasy is not just the expression of a controversy between the patient and any external object (extratransference), or between the patient and the analyst (transference), but between different conflictive parts of the patient within the innermost core of the self. It is really the struggle of the ego to establish its autonomy in dealing with opposite forces, split off, projected, and then unrecognized, experienced as foreign, unknown, and often frightening aspects of the self. In my experience, very often when interpretation is constructed emphasizing the intrapsychic conflict, there is usually a better understanding of the unconscious phantasy, because it helps the return of projection when decreasing superego sadism, diminishes the intensity of projective identification, and eases the way toward depressive mechanisms.

In general, I think that intrapsychic interpretation is relevant when dealing with at least three important transferential aspects: avoiding transference collusion in some borderline patients with perverse psychopathology; eluding the danger of persecutory anxiety when interpreting superego projections, also providing the ego with a proper perspective when dealing with the conflict; and interpreting self-envy mechanisms (López-Corvo 1992).

CLINICAL MATERIAL

Case 1

Nancy is a patient encountered previously.[1] She started the session talking about the previous one, in which according to her, I was against her having adventures.

---

[1]See page 157.

PT: Yesterday when I left I was very angry with you for what you said. I think that you were wrong, that it's very nice to get out of your office when you've been working the whole morning and go out for a picnic or something like that, or to travel and meet new people; nobody will ever take away from me the pleasure of seeing new faces or a new town, even my cousin (she refers to an extramarital affair that produced a great amount of anxiety and was one of her reasons for consulting) had a nice side.

TH: (While she speaks I feel the impact of the projective identification, that she is projecting in me an object that accuses her of doing things wrong, that having a good time is something forbidden.) I said: "You are trying to convince me as if you feel that I am the problem, the one who forbids you to get out of your office or to travel and meet new people, as if it is very difficult for you to think that perhaps it is you who also accuse yourself of doing whatever you might wish to do."

PT: When you were talking I remembered something and I didn't want to tell you, so I had to make an effort to say it to you. Once I was climbing the Avila[2] and L. told me that you cannot trust psychiatrists; that they have affairs with their patients; that they know how to do it so they don't get into trouble. I wonder if you might do the same. I guess that there might be many people who could do the same and don't feel bad about it. I wonder if my husband might do the same also.

_____
[2]A mountain in Caracas.

TH: There seems to be a serious confusion. If I were to have such power over you, then the solution to your guilt about having an affair would be for me to tell you how to do it in order not to get into trouble; or you could also question me, how could I pretend to reprimand you if I have no morals either, after all, I am doing exactly the same as you. (When I said this she laughed loudly.) In both circumstances you are providing me with a power over you that I don't have, as if it is difficult for you to acknowledge that you are really an adult, an independent person who can do whatever you wish to do; the problem is not really with me but between you and yourself.

PT: You have often insisted about this, that I place in you the power to control my behavior. I don't know exactly why it's always so difficult for me to see it, as if I prefer to make you so important. It doesn't matter how aware I am, I cannot help but feel that you could reprimand me for what I say or do and fear you as if you were my father. I wonder why. (Pause) I think it could be because I feel too lonely, that I prefer to be a child and to have a father or a mother than to have no one. It's like a hope—that you are so concerned about me that you will get angry over what I do. That's better than to feel that you're free to do as you please, but that you don't have anyone.

Case 2

Diana was a 35-year-old female patient, married to a very successful politician, and mother of two children. She worked as a researcher at the university. Diana was diagnosed as borderline with important narcissistic as well as paranoid features. In analysis for almost four years, four times a week, she had managed several achievements with her work and in relation to the harmony of her family: a closer relationship with her husband and the handling of her adolescent children. There was a difficult and painful history of early emotional deprivation, related to her parents' divorce when she was only 5 years old, after which her mother moved abroad, taking Diana and a younger sister with her. Later, when her mother could not keep Diana any longer at the house because of her work, she placed both daughters in a boarding school. At the age of 13 Diana moved back with her father who had married again and had two small children. She lived with them briefly until she was again sent to another boarding school where she remained until she was 16. She recalled those days with great anger and sadness particularly when she visited her father's house, and specifically at a time when her stepmother discovered that she had lice and forbade her to get close to anybody, especially her stepsisters. She remembered her feelings of humiliation, loneliness, desperation, and impotence while washing and drying her hair by herself, in order to clear up the infestation.

As the analysis progressed we referred to this hopeless and sad aspect in her as the "liced child," in contrast with another part that we alluded to as the "university professor," an important splitting that polarized the self and conditioned the transference–countertransference dimension. During weekend and holiday separations, she experienced the pain of abandonment and exclusion, resorting to manic defenses, such as leaving the country days before the holiday, abandoning the analysis in order to accompany her husband abroad, and bringing me expensive presents. All this behavior contrasted with her intense paranoid reaction the first time that I increased her fees, more than a year after the beginning of the analysis, in spite of a 30 percent inflation. Her anxiety was so extreme that she stopped the analysis for two weeks. A similar reaction occurred some time later, when her husband was removed from office and she became quite depressed. There was a need to preserve the splitting by continuously placing the "liced child" outside and keeping inside the expansive characteristics she felt were provided by the "university professor" part. The analysis could continue peacefully and gracefully if the fees were not increased, if I accepted her expensive presents, and if she was allowed to come and go as she pleased; in other words if I became the recipient, without any protest, of the projective identification of the "liced child," in order for her to feel completely certain that she was the powerful and triumphant "university professor." Any move toward reversing this mechanism elicited absolute terror.

During one session, it became clear that she was paying for her analysis with money from a grant she was receiving from a research institute. This, like the analysis, was a secondary activity, not important enough to warrant her primary interest; the analysis, in other words, was not her main concern. She produced a dream: *There was a guy, tall and slim, who had stolen something that looked like drugs, and who came to my house and gave me this drug with which I made a pyramid of yellow wax. It was radiant, a very pretty and graceful pyramid of around 40 centimeters in height and 10 square centimeters at the base. It reminded me of a building in downtown San*

Francisco. It was not like a flat Mayan pyramid, but long and tall. Then someone knocked on my door and there were some guys carrying a washing machine that was very good, a sort of new invention and they opened it. My house was in complete disorder, and I told them that I have another machine that I made myself, but it was very rudimentary. Its parts were tied with pieces of rope, but it could also work. Then I went outside with the pyramid and found a friend who is also a professor at the university, and gave him the pyramid and explained that it was made of a drug, and he said, "fantastic," took a piece from it, and said that he was going to use it in order to pay a debt. She provided few spontaneous associations, and when asked showed a tendency to idealize certain qualities, such as slim and elegant, or foreign, like San Francisco versus a Mayan pyramid. It appeared as if those qualities such as slim, elegant, radiant, and pretty were used to symbolize the idealized breast. But how, then, could we understand that such a beautiful pyramid was made out of drugs instead of gold or some other precious material? It seems as if her attempt to repair the breast, to change it into a beautiful pyramid-San Francisco-building, was also undermined, dirtied, like her apartment, by concealing stolen drugs inside. This reparatory attempt was repeated immediately after in the scene of the washing machines as an effort to clean the mess: there was the well-made machine brought by the visitors, a "new invention," and there was also the rudimentary machine that she made, not very sophisticated but working nevertheless. This scene was again followed by an envious attack, when she gave the pyramid to a friend who used it to pay his debt, representing her deceitfulness in paying for her analysis with a grant some institution had provided her for research, while at the same time continuously maintaining the fiction that she cannot afford more than a third of my fee. The interpretation of this last aspect generated an angry protest from Diana. "I cannot go around telling everybody how much I make because they might plunder me of what I have. Besides, I could never afford to pay you what you charge." But I felt that this was the opposite, and that via projective identification *she* was doing the plundering. I was the poor "liced child," while she was the rich "university professor." She argued angrily, saying that I was inventing theories that I wanted her to accept, that I was using her as a guinea pig, and, finally, as she had done many times before, she threatened to leave the analysis altogether. I felt that she was very intrigued by the hypotheses that I was producing with great concern in order to alleviate her suffering, but that a very envious aspect of herself was forcing her not to use any of them, not to recognize them as something of her own but to remain reluctant to use them, even if by doing so she could be helped. They were always "my theories" and never hers. Obviously we were dealing with the dynamic of a negative therapeutic reaction: the creative and repairing aspect of herself being constructed with my help was experienced as something foreign and attacked by another envious aspect of herself as a self-envy mechanism.

I said to her: "I wonder if this dream is also about what is taking place here between us, that there is a dishonest aspect in you that is trying to get rid of the 'liced child' by placing it in me, that there is a need to spoil the goodness, to make something important appear as irrelevant and dispensable. There is also an attempt to clean, not as well as the analytical-industrial washing machine, but with a homemade type of machine, capable of washing also." I felt that her need to preserve the plundered aspect outside and her anxiety about the failure of this projective defense made her feel that the problem was outside, between the two of us, instead of becoming aware that it was really an internal one, between her and herself, and related to the terror of having in the same place and at the same time the "plundered-liced-child" and the "rich-plundered-professor." I told her that an important aspect of the dream was the presence of a denouncer that helped us to see that inside the beautiful pyramid there was also something evil, a plunderer part, that tried to conceal the drug behind something beautiful. The problem was not that she could rob me, but that she robbed herself of knowing the truth.

There was a long silence, and finally she said that she had gone to the Research Institute, and was told that the closing date for her application was the following Friday. She told one of her associates not to tell anyone about it, as if she wanted nobody else to obtain a grant, "and it's so absurd to have such a desire, that nobody else could get a grant but me." It was easier to place the conflict outside instead of dealing with the envious part in her that wished to be the only child, and deceived her by making her believe that others wanted to plunder her, not to see or to use her homemade washer, as she was doing now, to clean the mess, the lie and deceit, and to become aware that the conflict was between two aspects of herself.

Case 3

At other times the choice might be between extratransference and intrapsychic interpretation, although this time the option is not determined by the danger of a perverse collusion but deals with the mechanism of projection, often used as defense against the superego's sadism. Antonio, the middle child of a family of three, is a young man who consulted originally because of certain difficulties with penile erection, which we have managed to associate, during one year of psychoanalytical treatment, with a very seductive and exhibitionist mother and a rather competitive father. He initiated the session by commenting about an argument he had with a university professor the day before, when some comments he made were unfairly disqualified by his teacher. He then remembered a similar dispute he had had with his father some time before, when he was asked to find out about the price of cellular telephones. His father tenaciously questioned the results of his inquiry, something that made Antonio so furious that he started to scream at his father, who got very angry also, to the point that he felt that they could have gotten into a fist fight or something of that sort. He associated both episodes, his teacher and his father, with competition over his mother when he was a child. I felt that there were several avenues here I could have used to structure the interpretation. To start, I saw no evidence of a transference projection, because I did not feel that I was disqualifying him or that he was particularly competing with me. Then I thought of an extratransference possibility, taking the direction of an oedipal rivalry and castration anxiety. However, I decided to take a different approach and to consider instead the mechanism of defense, in other words, the projection of part self-objects into the outside object. I said that perhaps his main difficulty was dealing with a "child element" inside of him that convinced him he was going to be a child forever, while at the same time making (projecting) or changing others into "powerful fathers" whose words he believed to have so much weight that he felt no way out of it but desperation.

Case 4

Another important aspect of intrapsychic interpretation is the possibility of dealing with superego projections, which can induce persecution and guilt when interpreted. Amelia is a 28-year-old housewife, in analysis for the last eight months, who consulted because of problems in her second marriage. She was the oldest of four sisters, and there was a history of resentment and sibling rivalry because she felt she always received the worst in her family. From very early on she was considered a "problem child" and was seen by a school psychologist around the fourth grade, accused of being verbally as well as physically abusive toward other children. Her adolescence was not easy either: she was rebellious, acted out frequently, had poor grades, and for a while used marijuana. When she was 18 she had to get married because she was pregnant, and was divorced shortly after giving birth to a girl who is now 10 years old. Currently she is seriously considering going back to the university; she is taking a course in economics and feels very happy about it: "Because it's different from before, now I am studying for myself instead of doing it to please my parents, as I used to do before." Two years ago she married again. Everything was going well until they started to have problems because "he is too jealous and I am too aggressive. We have too many discussions, and I don't want to get a divorce again." Amelia is a very attractive, coquettish, seductive, and intelligent young woman, always wearing very short skirts and low-necked dresses, as well as a generous amount of makeup. There is a dissociation in the transference between her exhibitionism and a feeling of low self-esteem; she fears being scolded, feels that she has nothing good to offer or to say, resulting in a certain difficulty in free associating. Countertransferentially, I am aware of her attractiveness, although her exhibitionism does not elicit any erotic feeling; but I feel that I should be cautious so as not to fall into the temptation of an exhibitionistic-voyeuristic couple.

During one of the first of her four sessions per week, she said: "This weekend I had a fight with my husband. Things had improved for a while, perhaps because I am less aggressive than before. This Saturday I was back from the university where I am taking a course in administration. He was watching TV. He was watching it the whole morning. Lately I try not to say anything about it, but I get very irritated when I see him like that, only watching TV, because he pays no attention to anything—the world could collapse and he wouldn't move. At the beginning, to catch his attention, I used to undress in front of the television. All he does is watch TV and TV and nothing else. Yesterday, I said that he looks like an idiot, with his mouth open and drooling, watching that stupid TV all day. I told him that he was going to become an imbecile, but he didn't answer me, and then I threw a mango I was eating and hit him on the head. He got furious and started to scream at me and then we insulted each other." Here she paused.

At this moment I decided to interpret, but was aware of the danger of inducing resistances, of incrementing the superego sadism, throwing a "mango" to her head, instead of helping her to gain insight, were I to say for instance, that she felt like a TV herself, that she wanted to compete with television, because what she really wanted was for all of us to drool while watching her, and that she felt very angry when this didn't happen. I decided to interpret in a different form: "Perhaps some anger that you feel against your husband is also against yourself, or better, against a powerful part inside you, which creates for you a real trap and great confusion, not knowing exactly what is more important for you, either "imbecilizing" yourself and changing into a TV, while changing all of us into "imbeciles," drooling while watching you, or using your head and your intelligence instead, which you are also trying to educate by bringing it to the university. Angry with being confused for not really knowing what is more important for you, your body or your head." She was silent for a short while and then she said: "I have never seen things in this way before."

By interpreting in this manner I was attempting to place the conflict inside, because her anger was not only about her husband preferring the TV to her, but also against herself, because of her need to compete with a television. Placing the conflict between two different parts of her self, I was also avoiding the danger of eliciting further superego sadism by inducing self-accusation if I were to identify only her unconscious transferential wish of competing with a TV. After all, this was not completely true either, because there was ambivalence in her. It was certain that a very important part of her was interested in a voyeuristic-exhibitionistic interaction, but there were other interests in her too. At the same time this interpretation attempted to provide the ego with a better perspective of the conflict, meaning that in the end the problem was the consequence of disparate and opposite interests continuously present within the self, trapping the ego between two different possibilities: either the conviction that being a TV and having everybody drooling over her was the real core of her oedipal revengeful hope, that is, winning over her mother for her father's complete attention, or, placing her full energy in developing other interests.

SUMMARY

There are certain borderline patients who present a perverse structure, often acted out in the analytical situation by means of intrusive projective identifications in order to foster a hidden, destructive, illegal, and narcissistic relationship with the analyst. The main purpose of this interaction is the creation of an avenging couple guided by a revengeful hope, which is sold by this organization to the ego, as the only exit from continuous suffering. This hope is based on a universal belief, or *basic delusion*, as I prefer to call it, that the mother is not autonomous and will always require the presence of the child in order to fulfill her narcissistic fault or penis envy. Such delusion, based on the disavowal of the mother's autonomy, is a way to deal with castration anxiety induced by the breaking of the natural symbiosis with the mother once mental space changes from complete narcissistic fulfillment to the painful appearance of exclusion during oedipal triangulation. In extreme cases the threat of castration introduced by reality induces these children to believe not that the mother is completely autonomous and does not require their presence in order to survive, making them non-essential, but that someone else (father, sibling, etc.) is already filling the mother's absence. The hope is then organized around the possibility of destroying that envied couple or unfair choice in order to establish the omnipotent dominion and control of the child again.

The intense pressure to create such a vengeful couple creates the need for a transference collusion or transference perversion by means of intense projective identification. In these particular circumstances, transference interpretation might be contraindicated because it could further induce the establishment of a perverse transference collusion. In order to avoid these complications interpretation needs to be directed to the inner aspects of the self.

Without dwelling on interpretations focused on extra-transference or transference situations, I am suggesting the possibility of intrapsychic interpretations as a third dimension, directed at the need to clarify the conflicted interaction of those split parts within the self, instead of aiming at the mechanism of projective identification.

Epilogue

This book opened with the question introduced by Scott (1975) about how difficult it has been for researchers in the field of mental health to account for mechanisms of self-envy, how a significant splitting or dissociation of the mind can often generate such an atmosphere of mental alienation and emotional estrangement, that a part of the self will deal with another aspect of that same self as if they were material from two different worlds. There is sometimes a tendency in both the mind and the body to deal with something familiar as if it was something new, distinct, and never before acknowledged, raising feelings of constant amazement and hopeful expectations. This tendency is the cornerstone of the "return of the repressed," of oedipal tragedy forever haunting and deceiving the ego that naively meets repressed derivatives as if they were completely new formulations. This mechanism is easily observed in narcissistic personalities who experience difficulty establishing lasting emotional relationships and resort to an endless collection of broken love affairs that imitate each other but that are always met with the thrill and expectation of a completely new infatuation. In some female patients this mechanism is reminiscent of Snow White's stepmother's mirror dilemma, indicating an unconscious and compulsive need to triangulate, to always assure the presence of another woman, and to use the male of that moment as the mirror, who, by either favoring or rejecting the other woman, will increase or dissolve the patient's inner suspicions that she is not the favored one. What is amazing about these cases is the naïveté displayed by the ego, always willing to be convinced that each new arrangement, or "Snow White complex," is completely different from any previous one.

In other words, it seems as if the process of splitting has the capacity to provide the splintered parts with a sort of new outfit that disguises them and renders them unrecognizable as something familiar. This is similar to the so-called autoimmune diseases, such as lupus erythematosus or diabetes, where cells equipped by the immune system to attack alien invaders assault sister cells with the same strength, unable to recognize in them an identical idiosyncrasy. In self-envy mechanism, early introjects, such as an envious-excluded child part, that remain trapped in the complicated conundrum of repressed memories, might not recognize new creative aspects of the same adult self, confusing them with narcissistic identifications once observed among adults, such as the loving harmony of the parents, mother's capacity to bear children, the tender parental attention toward other siblings, and so on. Perhaps the hypertrophy of the envious-excluded part in certain individuals could reach high levels of sensitivity in the presence of any of loving harmony and react strongly against it without being able to recognize that it is also a genuine part of the same self.

In her well-known article "Envy and Gratitude," Melanie Klein (1957) stated:

> My psycho-analytic experience has shown me that envy of creativeness is a fundamental element in the disturbance of the creative process. To spoil and destroy the initial source of goodness soon leads to destroying and attacking the babies that the mother contains and results in the good object being turned into a hostile, critical, and envious one. [p. 202]

Klein is referring here to feelings that arise from an envious inner object and are directed toward other persons. In self-envy, I am describing the same emotions, but instead of being directed against others in the outside world, they are experienced toward an introject, representing the creative part of the adult self, also confused with the creative aspects of the parents that were incorporated and narcissistically identified with as a child. What I am emphasizing now is the importance of the relationship between internal parts of the self in comparison with the interaction between the self and the external world. This is of great importance in psychoanalytical practice because the transference, in spite of its significance and usefulness, also represents a resistance that must be reduced if we expect the analysis to produce autonomy. The psychoanalytical setting is only an experimental situation, a laboratory where a transference neurosis or psychosis is cultivated in order for the analyst to properly acquire and understand basic knowledge of exactly how childhood events took place, in spite of all resistances, including screen memories. After all, mental disturbance has always proven to be the consequence of a space collapse that allows projection to take place, as well as a collapse of linear time, that makes transference and repetition compulsion a fact, and makes symbolization an impossible function. This is why any successful interpretation must add to the unconscious material three missing elements: time, space, and symbolism.

The importance of the interaction between the internal parts does not imply a polarization of both internal world and external reality, nor does it deprive transference of its ubiquitous relevance. On the contrary, its significance consists in a need to emphasize a purpose implicit in all psychoanalytical techniques: the resolution of infantile dependency by means of the working through of transference and the achievement of a functional ego autonomy. Interpretation of the self-envy mechanism requires the use of the form of intervention I have referred to as *intrapsychic interpretation*, described at length in the previous chapter. It is the emphasis given to the conflict between the parts. This strategy also introduces the symbolic space of the oedipal third occupied by the analyst at the moment of interpreting the conflict between the parts, which might also help to untie the narcissistic identifications used as material to manufacture projective identifications.

Self-envy is often observed among certain borderline patients, such as those with character disorders who resort to the use of acting out as a mean of destroying the parent's image of the idealized child, or in very creative individuals who present a serious level of suffering, providing a common combination of aesthetic creation and abundant psychopathology, usually bipolar and/or perverse.

In cases of negative therapeutic reaction, I find, sometimes, that an interpretation oriented toward the conflict between the parts might have more convincing force than a classical one directed to envy within the transference and related to the analyst. To show that the conflict is really located inside the self, "between you and you," as we might phrase it, will provide a better possibility for the ego's working alliance to participate, reducing also the temptation of negative transference, of directing aggression against objects projected inside the analyst; a situation that will help disentangle narcissistic identifications or the stuff employed to concoct projective identifications. However, there is always the risk of inducing superego attacks once we attempt to bring back persecutory elements into the self that have been projected with the purpose of creating a space between good and bad aspects of the self, a complication that the analyst should always keep in mind when attempting to interpret self-envy mechanisms or to stress the conflict between the parts.

In any case, the main purpose of this book is to provide a new perspective that might help in the very arduous task of reducing the level of suffering in very difficult patients.

References

Aray, J. (1985). *Senderos del Alma*. Caracas: Tropykos.

Bion, W. R. (1957). Differentiation of the psychotic from the non-psychotic personality. In *Second Thoughts: Selected Papers on Psychoanalysis*. London: Heinemann, 1967, pp. 43–64.

_____ (1959). Attacks on linking. In *Second Thoughts: Selected Papers on Psychoanalysis*. London: Heinemann, 1967, pp. 93–109.

_____ (1963). Elements of psycho-analysis. In *Seven Servants: Four Works by Wilfred Bion*, pp. 50–59. New York: Jason Aronson, 1977.

_____ (1967). *Second Thoughts: Selected Papers on Psychoanalysis*. London: Heinemann.

Bowlby, J. (1960). Grief and mourning in infancy and early childhood. Psychoanalytic Study of the Child, vol. 15. New York: International Universities Press.

Carder, S. L. (1991). Clinical case description of a segment of a psychoanalytic experience. *International Journal of Psycho-Analysis* 72:393–401.

Deutsch, H. (1942). Some forms of emotional disturbance and their relationship to schizophrenia. *Psychoanalytic Quarterly* 6. 11:301–321.

Ellman, R. (1982). *James Joyce.* New and Revised Edition. New York: Oxford University Press.

Emery, E. (1992). The envious eye: concerning some aspects of envy from Wilfred Bion to Harold Boris. *Melanie Klein and Object Relations.* 10:19.

Fairbairn, W.R.D. (1952). *Psychoanalytic Studies of the Personality.* London: Tavistock.

Ferenczi, S. (1933). Confusion of tongues between adults and child. In *Final Contributions to the Problem of Methods of Psycho-analysis,* ed. M. Balint, trans. E. Masbacher and others. New York: Basic Books, 1955.

Freud, A., and Burlingham, D. (1944) *Infants without Family.* New York: International Universities Press.

Freud, S. (1893). On the psychical mechanism of hysterical phenomena. *Standard Edition* 3:25.

_____ (1894). Neuro-psychoses of defense. *Standard Edition* 3:41.

_____ (1908). Creative writers and daydreaming. *Standard Edition* 9:141.

_____ (1910). Leonardo da Vinci and a memory of his childhood. *Standard Edition* 11:59.

_____ (1911). Psychoanalytic notes on an autobiographical account of a case of paranoia (dementia paranoides) *Standard Edition* 12:1.

_____ (1913). The theme of the three caskets. *Standard Edition* 12:289.

_____ (1914). On narcissism: an introduction. *Standard Edition* 14:67.

____ (1915). Repression. *Standard Edition* 14:141.

____ (1916). Some character types met with in psychoanalytic work. *Standard Edition.* 14:309.

____ (1917a). On transformations of instinct as exemplified in anal erotism. *Standard Edition.* 17:125.

____ (1917b). Mourning and melancholia. *Standard Edition.* 14:237.

____ (1920). Beyond the pleasure principle. *Standard Edition.* 18:1.

____ (1923). The ego and the id. *Standard Edition.* 19:1.

____ (1924a). Neurosis and psychosis. *Standard Edition.* 19:149.

____ (1924b). The economic problem of masochism. *Standard Edition* 19:155

____ (1926). Inhibition symptoms and anxiety. *Standard Edition.* 20:75.

____ (1927). Fetishism. *Standard Edition.* 21:147.

____ (1930). Civilization and its discontents. Standard Edition. 21:57.

____ (1940a). An outline of psychoanalysis. *Standard Edition.* 23:139.

____ (1940b). Splitting of the ego in the process of defense. *Standard Edition.* 23:271.

____ (1950). Extracts from the Fliess papers. *Standard Edition* 1:220–228 (1892–1899).

Gay, P. (1988) *Freud: A Life for Our Time.* New York: Norton.

Gill, M. M. (1982). *The Analysis of Transference*, vol. 1, *Theory and Technique.* Psychological Issues, Monograph 53. New York: International Universities Press.

Green, A. (1975). Orestes and Oedipus. *International Review of Psycho-Analysis* 2:355.

Greenacre, P. (1960). Further notes on fetishism In *Emotional Growth: Psychoanalytic Studies of the Gifted and a Great Variety of Other Individuals. Volume I.* New York: International Universities Press, 1971, p. 182.

_____ (1968). Perversion: general considerations regarding their genetic and dynamic background. In *Emotional Growth*: vol. I. *Psychoanalytic Studies of the Gifted and a Great Variety of Other Individuals.* New York: International Universities Press, 1971, p. 300.

Grinberg, L. (1957). Perturbaciones en la interpretación motivadas por la contraidentificación protectiva. Revista de Psicoanálisis 14:1–12.

_____ (1976). *Teoría de la Identificación.* Buenos Aires: Editorial Paidos.

Grosskurth, P. (1990). *Melanie Klein: Her World and Her Work.* London: Hodder and Stoughton.

Grotstein, J. S. (1986). *Splitting and Projective Identification.* New York: Jason Aronson.

Guntrip, H. (1969). *Schizoid Phenomena, Object Relations, and the Self.* New York: International Universities Press.

Hartmann, H. (1964). *Essays on Ego Psychology.* New York: International Universities Press.

Heimann, P. (1950) On counter-transference. *International Journal of Psycho-Analysis.* 31:81–84.

Jacobson, E. (1964). *The Self and the Object World.* New York: International Universities Press.

Joseph, B. (1975). The patient who is difficult to reach. In *Tactics and Techniques in Psychoanalytic Therapy, vol. 2, Countertransference*, ed. P. L. Giovacchini, pp. 205–216. New York: Jason Aronson.

____ (1989). *Psychic Equilibrium and Psychic Change.* London: Tavistock.

Kanner, L. (1944). Early infantile autism. *Journal of Pediatrics* 25:211–217.

Kernberg, O. (1975). *Borderline Conditions and Pathological Narcissism.* New York: Jason Aronson.

____ (1989). An ego psychology object relations theory of the structure and treatment of pathologic narcissism. *Psychiatric Clinics of North America* 12:(3) 723.

Khan, M. (1974). *The Privacy of the Self.* New York: International Universities Press.

Klein, M. (1932). *The Psychoanalysis of Children.* New York: Delacorte, 1975.

____ (1940). Mourning and its relations to manic depressive states. *International Journal of Psycho-Analysis.* 21:125–153.

____ (1946). Notes on some schizoid mechanisms. In *Envy and Gratitude.* 1990. London: Virago, p. 1.

____ (1952). The origins of transference. *International Journal of Psycho-Analysis* 433–438.

____ (1957). Envy and gratitude. In *Envy and Gratitude,* 1990. London: Virago, p. 176.

____ (1963). Some reflections on the *Oresteia.* In *Envy and Gratitude.* London: Virago, p. 275.

Klein, S. (1980). Autistic phenomena in neurotic patients. *International Journal of Psycho-Analysis* 61:395–407.

Kohut, H. (1971). *The Analysis of the Self.* New York: International Universities Press.

____ (1977). *The Restoration of the Self.* New York: International Universities Press.

Kris, A. (1976). On wanting too much: the "exceptions"

revisited. *International Journal of Psycho-Analysis* 57:85–95.

Ladan, A. (1992). On the secret fantasy of being an exception. *International Journal of Psycho-Analysis* 73: 29–38.

Laplanche, J., and Pontalis, J. B. (1973). *The Language of Psychoanalysis*, London: Hogarth.

López-Corvo, R. E. (1990). *Adictos y Adicciones.* Caracas: Monte Avila.

——— (1992). About interpretation of self-envy. *International Journal of Psycho-Analysis* 73:719–728.

——— (1993). A Kleinian understanding of addiction. *Melanie Klein and Object Relations* 11:1–94.

Mahler, M. (1952). On child psychoses and schizophrenia: autistic and symbiotic infantile psychoses. *Psychoanalytic Study of the Child* 7:286–305. New York: International Universities Press.

——— (1972a). On the first three subphases of the separation-individuation process. In *Selected Papers,* vol. 2. New York: Jason Aronson.

——— (1972b). Rapprochement subphase of the separation-individuation process. In *Selected Papers*, vol. 2. New York: Jason Aronson.

Meltzer, D. (1966). The relation of anal masturbation to projective identification. *International Journal of Psycho-Analysis* 47:335–342.

——— (1967). *The Psycho-Analytic Process.* London: Heinemann.

——— (1973). *Sexual States of the Mind.* Perthshire, Scotland: Clunie.

Meltzer, D., Bremner, J., Hoxter, S., et al. (1975). *Explorations in Autism.* Perthshire, Scotland: Clunie.

McGuire, W. (1974). *The Freud-Jung Letters*. London: Hogarth.

Piaget, J. (1961). La formación del símbolo en el niño. Mexico: Fondo de Cultura Económica.

_____ (1971). *Biology and Knowledge*. Chicago: University of Chicago Press.

Racker, H. (1953). Contribution to the problem of counter-transference. *International Journal of Psycho-Analysis* 38:4–10.

Rosenfeld, H. (1952). Transference-phenomena and transference-analysis in an acute catatonic schizophrenic patient. In *Psychotic States*. (1965) New York: International Universities Press.

_____ (1971). A clinical approach to the psychoanalytic theory of life and death instincts. *International Journal of Psycho-Analysis* 52:169.

Sabato, E. (1975). Informe sobre ciegos. In *Sobre Heroes y Tumbas*. Buenos Aires: Editorial Sudamericana.

Scott, W. C. M. (1975). Self-envy and envy of dreams and dreaming. *International Review of Psycho-Analysis* 2:333.

Segal, H. (1964). *Introduction to the Work of Melanie Klein*. New York: Basic Books.

_____ (1981). *The Work of Hanna Segal: A Kleinian Approach to Clinical Practice*. New York: Jason Aronson.

_____ (1983). Some clinical implications of M. Klein's work. *International Journal of Psycho-Analysis* 64:269.

_____ (1993). On the clinical usefulness of the concept of death instinct. *International Journal of Psycho-Analysis* 74:55.

Shengold, L. L., (1979). Child abuse and deprivation: soul

murder. *Journal of the American Psychoanalytic Association.* 27:539–559.

Spielrein, S. (1912). Die Destruktion als Ursache des Werdens. (Destruction as the cause of becoming). *Jahrbuch für Psychoanalytische und Psychopathologische Forschungen* 4:465–503.

Steele, B. R., and Pollock, C. B. (1968). A psychiatry study of parents who abuse infants and small children. In *Battered Child,* ed. F. E. Helfer and C. H. Kempe. Chicago: University of Chicago Press.

Steiner, J. (1981). Perverse relationships between parts of the self. *International Journal of Psycho-Analysis.* 62:241.

Thigpen, C. H., and Cleckley, H. M. (1958). *The Three Faces of Eve.* New York: McGraw-Hill.

Tustin, F. (1972). *Autism and Childhood Psychoses.* London: Hogarth.

Van Waning, A. (1992). Pioneering psychoanalyst Sabina Spielrein. *International Review of Psycho-Analysis.* 19:399.

Waddington, C. H. (1957). *The Strategy of the Genes: A Discussion of Aspects of Theoretical Biology.* London: Allen & Unwin.

Winnicott, D. (1951). Transitional objects and transitional phenomena. In *Playing and Reality,* pp. 1–25. New York: Basic Books, 1971.

——— (1960a). *Ego Distortion in Terms of True and False Self.* New York: International Universities Press, pp. 140–152.

——— (1960b). The theory of the parent–infant relationship. In *The Maturational Processes and the Facilitating*

Environment, pp. 37–55. New York: International Universities Press.

Wisdom, J. O. (1961). A methodological approach to the problem of hysteria. *International Journal of Psycho-Analysis* 42:120–130.

Wolfenstein, M. (1969). Loss, rage, and repetition. *Psychoanalytic Study of the Child*, vol. 24. New York: International Universities. Press.

Yallop, D. (1984). *In God's Name*. London: Poetic Products.

Index

Acting out, self-envy and,
    borderline personality,
    176–181
Action, destructive
    narcissism, 102–103
Adler, A., 115
Aggression
  destructive narcissism, 97
  libido compared and
    contrasted, 113–122
  masochism, self-envy and,
    148
  projection and, 64–65
Amyotrophic lateral sclerosis, 9
Anger, breast and, 65
Anus, borderline personality,
    156, 157
Anxiety, autoeroticism,
    omnipotent object control,
    86
Aray, J., 95
Aristotle, 10, 45n2, 80n2

Atlas complex, 86
Autism
  obsessive defenses, 68–70
  schizoid phenomena, 64
  trauma and, 51–52
Autoeroticism
  hope (revengeful versus
    depressive), 132,
    138–139
  omnipotent object control,
    threats to, schizoid
    phenomena, 86
Avoidance mechanisms,
    schizoid phenomena,
    mother–child symbiosis,
    cultural factors, 73–85

Bad breast. *See also* Breast;
  Good breast
  mother–child relationship
    and, 65
  splitting and, 50

Bad object
  destructive narcissism,
    91–92
  hope (revengeful versus
    depressive), 128
Beethoven, Ludwig van, 6, 8
Biology
  epigenesis, destructive
    narcissism, 93–94, 95
  hope (revengeful versus
    depressive), 129
Bion, W. R., 30, 31, 38, 50,
  51, 54, 63, 64, 69, 71, 75,
  79, 102, 188
Bleuler, E., 31
Borderline personality,
  147–181
  acting out and self-envy,
    176–181
  case examples, 150–176
  hope (revengeful versus
    depressive), 128,
    129–130, 131–144
  interpretation, 204–205
  schizoid phenomena, 64
  self-envy and, 147–151,
    210–211
  splitting and, 51
Borges, Jorge Luis, 5, 8
Bowlby, J., 67
Breast. *See also* Bad breast;
  Good breast
  autoeroticism, omnipotent
    object control, threats
    to, schizoid phenomena,
    86
  destructive narcissism, 92

integration and, 54, 69–70
mother–child relationship
  and, 65
splitting and, 50
Breuer, J., 32
Burlingham, D., 67

Calder, S., 117, 119, 121
Castration anxiety, hope
  (revengeful versus
  depressive), 130, 132
Child molestation, case
  history, 14
Children, cognitive splitting,
  normal, 48–49
Cleckley, H. M., 58
Cognitive development,
  splitting and, 43–44
Cognitive splitting, normal,
  48–49
Continent mother, projection
  and, 64
Countertransference
  borderline personality, 153
  case history, 15, 18–19, 40
  hope (revengeful versus
    depressive), 131, 132,
    134, 143
  resistance and, 85
  schizoid phenomena, 65–66
Creativity
  breast and, 65
  envy and, 209
  psychopathology and, 12
  self-envy and
    mental state and, 10–22
    physical ailment, 3–9

Crime, destructive narcissism, 103

Cultural factors, mother–child relationship, schizoid phenomena, 68–87

Cumulative trauma, obsessive defenses, 70–73

Daydreaming, creativity and, 11

Death instinct
  destructive narcissism, 100
  psychoanalytic theory and, 114–117

Defenses
  dismantling, splitting and, 51–52
  hope (revengeful versus depressive), 130, 135–136
  obsessive, 68–73
    autism, 68–70
    cumulative trauma, 70–73
  repression and, 36
  splitting and, 30–31, 32, 64

Delusion, hope (revengeful versus depressive), 127–131

Demosthenes, 80n2

Depersonalization, schizoid phenomena, 66

Depression, schizoid phenomena, mother–child symbiosis, disturbed, 66–67

Depressive hope, revengeful hope verus, 127–144. *See also* Hope (revengeful versus depressive)

Depressive position, splitting and, 49–50

Derealization, schizoid phenomena, 66

Destructive narcissism, 91–109
  clinical confusion, 95–98
  described, 91–92
  fusion and idealization, 98–100
  hope (revengeful versus depressive), 127–128, 130–131
  perverse narcissism and, 100–109
  psychoanalytic theory, 92–95

Determinism, epigenesis, destructive narcissism, 94

Deutsch, H., 63, 67, 130

Developmental factors. *See* Cognitive development

Disavowal, repression and, 36–37

Dismantling
  culture and, 70
  schizoid secret, 80
  splitting and, 51–52

Dissociative state, splitting and, 47–48

Dream analysis
  borderline personality, 154–155, 156

Dream analysis (*continued*)
hope (revengeful versus
depressive), 133,
134–135, 137, 139–140,
141, 142, 143–144
mother–child relationship,
eye contact, narcissistic
fusion and, 20–21
penis, integration and,
54–55
unconscious fantasy and,
xi–xii
Drug abuse, destructive
narcissism, 103

Ego
cognitive splitting and, 48
culture and, 69
destructive narcissism, 93,
94–95, 96, 97
hope (revengeful versus
depressive), 127–128,
129, 139–140
ideal object, reparation and,
13
self-envy compared and
contrasted, 23
splitting, 35, 38. *See also*
Splitting
integration and, 53–54
self-envy and, 29, 149
Ego psychology, psycho-
analytic theory, 113–114
Eleusinian Mysteries, 79–80
Ellmann, R., 5
Emery, E., 123

Envy
breast and, 65
creativity and, 209
described, 29–30
Oedipus complex and,
122–124
phallic envy, culture and, 69
self-envy and, 30
Epigenesis, destructive
narcissism, 93–94, 95
Essentiality, omnipotent
object control, threats to,
schizoid phenomena, 87
Exception, hope (revengeful
versus depressive),
127–131
Exhibitionism. *See*
Narcissistic exhibitionism
Extratransference
interpretation, described,
185. *See also*
Interpretation

Fairbairn, W. R. D., 38, 45,
64, 100
False self
schizoid phenomena,
mother–child symbiosis,
phobic and avoidance
mechanisms, 75
splitting, nothingness and
otherness, 55–58
Family dynamics, destructive
narcissism, 103
Fantasy. *See also*
Unconscious fantasy
borderline personality, 153

hope (revengeful versus depressive), 132
Feces, penis and, hope (revengeful versus depressive), 130
Fenichel, O., 121
Ferenczi, S., 67
Fetishism
  omnipotent object control, threats to, schizoid phenomena, 86
  repression and, 36–37
  splitting and, 33–34
Fliess, W., 35
Freud, A., 67, 121
Freud, S., xi, 10–11, 22, 23, 31, 32, 33, 34–36, 37, 44, 45, 68, 70, 87, 94, 95–96, 97, 99, 114–117, 121, 122, 147, 148, 190
Fusion, idealization and, destructive narcissism, 98–100

Gay, P., 114, 115
Gill, M. M., 186
Good breast. *See also* Bad breast; Breast
  integration and, 54
  mother–child relationship and, 65
  splitting and, 50
Good-enough fathering, integration and, 55
Good-enough mothering
  integration and, 54
  projection and, 64

Good object
  destructive narcissism, 91–92
  hope (revengeful versus depressive), 128
Grandiose self, destructive narcissism, 97
Green, A., 124
Greenacre, P., 67
Grinberg, L., 85
Grosskurth, P., 122
Grotstein, J. S., 30, 44, 46–47, 54, 55
Guilt
  autoeroticism, omnipotent object control, threats to, schizoid phenomena, 86
  self-envy compared and contrasted, 23
Guntrip, H., 64–66, 67

Hallucinogens, 80n2
Hartmann, H., 71, 97
Hawking, Stephen, 9
Heimann, P., 85
Holding environment, splitting and, 53–54
Homer (Greek poet), 5
Homosexuality, borderline personality, self-envy and acting out, 179–181
Hope (revengeful versus depressive), 127–144
  case example, 131–144
  delusion and indispensability, 127–131

Horizontal splitting, vertical splitting and, 38–43. *See also* Splitting

Iatrogenic splitting, described, 58–59
Idealization, fusion and, destructive narcissism, 98–100
Ideal object
destructive narcissism, 99–100
reparation and, 12–13
splitting, nothingness and otherness, 55–59
Indispensability, hope (revengeful versus depressive), 127–131
Infancy, cognitive development and, 43–44
Infantile sexuality, psychoanalytic theory and, 115
Integration, splitting and, 53–55
Internal representation, splitting and, 44–46
Interpretation, 185–205
borderline personality generally, 204–205, 210–211
self-envy and, 150
case examples, 192–204
phases of, 185–192
Intrapsychic interpretation, described, 186–187. *See also* Interpretation

Intrauterine interaction
destructive narcissism, 95
mother–child relationship, 64
Introjection
destructive narcissism, 99–100
self-envy and, 30, 209
Introjective identification
hope (revengeful versus depressive), 136
projective identification and, xii–xiii
self-envy and, borderline personality, 150
splitting and, 47

Jacobson, E., 96, 97
Janet, P., 31, 32
John Paul I (pope of Rome), 3–4, 8
Joseph, B., 63, 120, 190
Joyce, James, 5, 8
Jung, C. G., 114–115

Kanner, L., 68, 69
Kerenyi, K., 80n2
Kernberg, O., xi, 49, 97–98, 99
Khan, M., 68, 70, 71, 73n1
Klein, M., 11, 22–23, 31, 37, 46, 47, 50, 53, 54, 64, 95, 98–99, 100, 109, 121, 122, 124, 147, 209
Klein, S., 68
Kohut, H., 11, 38–39, 43, 97
Kris, A., 121, 190

Ladan, A., 190
Laplanche, J., 93, 117
Libidinal narcissism
  described, 95–96
  destructive narcissism
    compared, 91, 99
Libido
  aggression compared and
    contrasted, 113–122
  death instinct and, 114
Loewenstein, R. M., 121
López-Corvo, R. E., 130, 189,
  192
Luciani, Albino. *See* John
  Paul I (pope of Rome)

Macroscopic splitting,
  described, 47
Mahler, M., 68, 76
Marcus Aurelius, 80n2
Masochism, self-envy and, 148
Masturbation. *See*
  Autoeroticism
McGuire, W., 115n1
Melancholy, poetry and, 10–11
Meltzer, D., 33, 51, 63, 64, 68,
  69, 70, 105, 130, 150,
  190, 191
Microscopic splitting,
  described, 47
Monte Cristo paradigm, 102,
  128
Mother–child relationship
  breast, splitting and, 50
  eye contact, narcissistic
    fusion and, 14–22

holding environment, 54
hope (revengeful versus
  depressive), 128
projection and, 64
schizoid phenomena. *See
  also* Schizoid
  phenomena
  cultural factors, 68–87
  disturbed, 66–67
Multiple personality,
  iatrogenic splitting, 58–59

Narcissism, destructive,
  91–109. *See also*
  Destructive narcissism
Narcissistic exhibitionism,
  creativity and, 11, 12–13
Narcissistic personality
  hope (revengeful versus
    depressive), 128
  schizoid phenomena, 64
  splitting and, 49–50
Normal schizo-paranoid
  position, breast and, 65
Nothingness, otherness and,
  splitting, 55–59

Object relations theory
  destructive narcissism,
    101–102
  self-envy and, xi
  splitting and, 43–46
Obsessive defenses, 68–73
  autism, 68–70
  cumulative trauma, 70–73
  schizoid secret, 80

Oedipus complex
  destructive narcissism, 108
  integration and, 55
  psychoanalysis and, 147
  return of the repressed, 207
  revenge and, 122–124
  splitting, case history,
    41–43
Omnipotent object control,
  threats to, schizoid
  phenomena, mother–child
  symbiosis, cultural
  factors, 86–87
Otherness, nothingness and,
  splitting, 55–59

Paranoid-schizoid position,
  destructive narcissism,
  100
Pathological schizo-paranoid
  position, breast and, 65
Penis
  anus/vagina, borderline
    personality, 156–157
  homosexuality, borderline
    personality, self-envy
    and acting out, 179–181
  hope (revengeful versus
    depressive), 128,
    129–130
  integration and, 54–55
  phallic envy, culture and,
    69
Perverse narcissism,
  destructive narcissism
  and, 100–109
Phobic mechanisms, schizoid
  phenomena, mother–child

symbiosis, cultural
  factors, 73–85
Piaget, J., 29, 48, 49, 93–94
Plato, 80n2
Play behavior, creativity and,
  11
Poetry, melancholy and,
  10–11
Pollock, C. B., 67
Pontalis, J. B., 93, 117
Primary narcissism,
  described, 96
Projection
  envy and, 30
  hope (revengeful versus
    depressive), 135–136
  splitting and, 64–65
Projective identification
  hope (revengeful versus
    depressive), 129, 136
  introjective identification
    and, xii–xiii
  self-envy and, borderline
    personality, 150
  splitting and, 47
Prostitution, destructive
  narcissism, 103
Psychic trauma. See Trauma
Psychoanalytic theory
  destructive narcissism,
    92–95
  ego psychology, 113–114
  interpretation and, 185
  libido and aggression,
    compared and
    contrasted, 113–122
  Oedipus complex and,
    122–124, 147

splitting and, 31, 32–35
unconscious and, 11
Psychogenic autism. *See*
Autism
Psychopathology
creativity and, 12
splitting and, 30
normal splitting compared,
46–52
Psychosis
schizoid phenomena,
63–87. *See also*
Schizoid phenomena
splitting and, 30, 33–34, 38
splitting of time and, 52–53

Racker, H., 85
Rat Man case (Freud), 33–34
Religion, cognitive splitting,
normal, 48
Reparation
creativity and self-envy,
10–22
sublimation and, 11
Repression
splitting and, 11
splitting compared and
contrasted, 35–43,
45–46
Resistance
countertransference and, 85
slips and, xii
Return of the repressed,
Oedipus complex, 207
Revenge
interpretation, 188–189
Oedipus complex and,
122–124

Revengeful hope, depressive
hope verus, 127–144. *See
also* Hope (revengeful
versus depressive)
Reversible perspective,
splitting and, 51
Rheumatoid arthritis, 9
Rosenfeld, H., 63, 85, 91, 96,
107, 108, 128, 187, 191

Sabato, Ernesto, 5
Schizoid phenomena, 63–87
described, 63–66
mother–child symbiosis
cultural factors, 68–87
obsessive defenses,
68–73
omnipotent object
control, threats to,
86–87
phobic and avoidance
mechanisms, 73–85
disturbed, 66–67
schizoid secret, 79–86
Schizoid secret, described,
79–86
Schizo-paranoid position,
breast and, 65
Schreber, D. P., 73, 96
Scott, W. C. M., xi, 23–24, 47,
149, 207
Secondary narcissism,
described, 96–97
Segal, H., 11, 12, 37, 98, 109,
121
Self-envy
acting out and, borderline
personality, 176–181

Self-envy (*continued*)
  borderline personality and,
    147–181, 210–211.
    See also Borderline
    personality
  case example, 6–8
  creativity and
    mental state and, 10–22
    physical ailments, 3–9
  envy and, 30
  interpretation, 185–205.
    See also Interpretation
  introjection and, 209
  object relations theory and,
    xi
  self-reproach compared
    and contrasted,
    22–26
  splitting and, 29
Self-object
  dream analysis and, xii
  hope (revengeful versus
    depressive), 128
Self-reproach, self-envy
    compared and contrasted,
    22–26
Separation anxiety, hope
    (revengeful versus
    depressive), 136
Sexual fantasy, borderline
    personality, 153
Shengold, L. L., 67, 73
Slips, resistance and, xii
Spielrein, S., 114–115, 116
Splitting
  Freudian view of, 29–35
  iatrogenic, 58–59
  integration and, 53–55

normal and
    psychopathological,
    46–52
  nothingness and otherness,
    55–59
  object relations theory and,
    43–46
  psychopathology and, 30
  repression and, 11
  repression compared and
    contrasted, 35–43
  schizoid phenomena,
    63–87. *See also*
    Schizoid phenomena
  of time, 52–53
  unconscious fantasy and,
    xii–xiii
Steel, B. R., 67
Steiner, J., 102, 151, 187,
    190
Strachey, J., 31n1
Sublimation
  creativity and, 13–14
  reparation and, 11
Success, self-envy and,
    22–23
Superego
  self-envy compared and
    contrasted, 23, 24
  splitting and, 33

Tancredo Neves, Almeida de,
    4–5, 8
Thigpen, C. H., 58
Time, splitting of, 52–53
Transference
  case history, 40

hope (revengeful versus
    depressive), 128, 143
interpretation, 190
mother–child relationship,
    eye contact, narcissistic
    fusion and, 21–22
omnipotent object control,
    threats to, schizoid
    phenomena, 86–87
schizoid phenomena,
    65–66
Transference interpretation,
    described, 185–186. *See
    also* Interpretation
Trauma
    autism and, 51–52
    cognitive development and,
        44
    cumulative trauma,
        obsessive defenses,
        70–73
    splitting and, 49–50
True self, splitting,
    nothingness and
    otherness, 55–58
Tustin, F., 64, 68

Unconscious, psychoanalytic
    theory and, 11
Unconscious fantasy. *See also*
    Fantasy
    borderline personality,
        self-envy and, 150
    creativity and, 11
    dream analysis and, xi–xii
    hope (revengeful versus
        depressive), 129–130
    splitting and, xii–xiii

Vagina, borderline
    personality, 156, 157
Vertical splitting, horizontal
    splitting and, 38–43. *See
    also* Splitting

Waddington, C. H., 94
Wallerstein, R., 117
Winnicott, D. W., 11, 50, 53,
    54, 55–56, 63, 64, 71,
    130, 148–149
Wisdom, J. O., 30

Yallop, D., 4